D1077191

*O*ther titles in the **Young Pathfinder** *series*

Working together: Native speaker assistants in the primary school (YPF12)
Cynthia Martin and Anne Farren

A flying start!: Introducing early language learning (YPF11)
Peter Satchwell and June de Silva

A world of languages: Developing children's love of languages (YPF10)
Manjula Datta and Cathy Pomphrey

The literacy link (YPF9)
Catherine Cheater and Anne Farren

Grammar is fun (YPF8)
Lydia Biriotti

Making the link: Relating languages to other work in the school (YPF7)
Daniel Tierney and Malcolm Hope

Let's join in! Rhymes, poems and songs (YPF6)
Cynthia Martin and Catherine Cheater

First steps to reading and writing (YPF5)
Christina Skarbek

Keep talking: Teaching in the target language (YPF4)
Peter Satchwell

Are you sitting comfortably?: Telling stories to young language learners (YPF3)
Daniel Tierney and Patricia Dobson

Games and fun activities (YPF2)
Cynthia Martin

CILT, the National Centre for Languages, seeks to support and develop multilingualism and intercultural competence among all sectors of the population in the UK.

CILT serves education, business and the wider community with:

- specialised and impartial information services;
- high quality advice and professional development;
- expert support for innovation and development;
- quality improvement in language skills and service provision.

CILT is a charitable trust, supported by the DfES and other Government departments throughout the UK.

early language learning

ELL is a DfES initiative managed by CILT, the National Centre for Languages, working in partnership with QCA, BECTA, the British Council Education and Training Group, the TDA, OFSTED and the Association for Language Learning.

Young Pathfinder 13

A CILT series for primary language teachers

Mind the gap!

Improving transition between Key Stage 2 and 3

Rosemary Bevis and Ann Gregory

The views expressed in this publication are the authors' and do not necessarily represent those of CILT.

Acknowledgements

Rosemary and Ann would like to express their gratitude for the support they have received from their families, colleagues and friends, as well as all the pupils and teachers who have influenced their understanding of primary language learning over the years. They would particularly like to thank:

John Bevis, Catherine Cheater, Therese Comfort, Judi Fairbanks, Sue Gardiner, Gerry Gregory, Judy Hawker, Eric Hawkins, Ros Hopwood, Jim McElwee, Pat McLagan, Cynthia Martin, Kirsty Pierce, Sue Snow, David Stork, Doris Sygmund and Dan Tierney; the Tameside PRISM Team; fellow members of the Early Language Learning Advisory Forum; colleagues involved in the Good Practice and Best Practice projects, especially in Stockport and York; pupils and staff at Aylesbury High School; pupils and staff in Wythenshawe, Liverpool, Richmond upon Thames, South Gloucestershire, Northumberland, East Riding of Yorkshire and North Yorkshire; past and present students and staff at York St John College; CILT staff and all those whose excellent work has been referred to in this book.

The authors and publisher would like to thank those who granted permission to reproduce copyright material.

Contents

Introduction

[We should] view the transition to secondary schooling as part of a coherent whole, rather than thinking in terms of separate primary then secondary programmes.

(Martin 2000)

Transition between Key Stages can be problematic in any curriculum area, but it is potentially more so in early language learning as not all children currently have similar experiences. Since language learning is to become an entitlement for primary pupils by 2010 it is essential that the issues of transition be addressed, especially between Years 6 and 7. As more children learn a foreign language in primary school, similar issues of continuity and progression may also exist at the point of transfer between Key Stages 1 and 2. Although the main focus of this book is the transition point from Key Stage 2 to Key Stage 3, pupils will have already made one transition from Key Stage 1 to Key Stage 2, when their teachers tried to ensure that prior knowledge and skills were recognised and built on. A similar acknowledgement of prior learning must be assured from Key Stages 2 to 3.

Communication between teachers of languages in primary and secondary schools is crucial to ensuring successful continuity and progression in language learning.

This *Young Pathfinder* aims to help bridge the gap between the primary and secondary phases, to establish and maintain continuity and progression, and to aid effective transition for your pupils. We suggest how teachers can explore their common problems and we provide practical ideas for activities, joint events and methodology, which can help reinforce the smooth progression of skills, especially between Key Stages 2 and 3. As French is the language most commonly taught in primary schools, most examples given are in French, although all the activities can easily be adapted to other languages.

The book is structured as follows:

* Chapters 1 and 2 focus on how teachers in primary and secondary schools can get to know each other, developing effective liaison and joint planning;
* Chapter 3 deals with transfer of information and assessment: the difference between them and how they can be achieved;
* Chapter 4 describes projects which can support continuity and progression, including Primary Languages Days and other special events, which can be run by the primary schools, or be run jointly with secondary partners;
* Chapter 5 presents detailed plans for running such a joint primary–secondary project (supported by sample materials in Appendix 2);
* Chapter 6 suggests methodology and activities for Year 7 classes with mixed levels in the foreign language;
* information is provided in Appendix 1 on sources of support and networks which aim to build bridges between all the different people involved in the transition process.

THE CURRENT SITUATION

While the exact situation regarding the number of children currently learning a foreign language is not known, various research projects have indicated general trends, suggesting an increase in primary languages even before the *National Languages Strategy* (DfES 2002) was announced. The most recent study indicates that 43% of primary children are currently learning a foreign language at Key Stage 2, either in class or as an extra-curricular activity (Driscoll, Jones and Macrory 2004).

The increasing availability of resources, support and training opportunities is leading to a continuing increase in provision in primary schools, with the consequence of a greater acknowledgement of prior learning by secondary colleagues.

DIVERSITY OF PROVISION

Currently, the nature of teaching can vary from school to school and sometimes from class to class within the same school. In some schools a foreign language is introduced in Reception, in others it is introduced only in Year 6. It can range from whole-school timetabled classes taught by specialists to occasional one-off lessons taught by an enthusiastic parent; from regular input by peripatetic secondary colleagues to literacy-linked projects or private language clubs. This diversity of provision gives rise to concerns and challenges about progression from Key Stage 2. If there is to be effective transition between Key Stages 2 and 3 it is important to establish an efficient and accurate transfer of information and to build on prior skills and knowledge. In some secondary schools there is clear differentiation in Year 7; in others no account is taken of any prior language-learning experiences. In some schools, information is passed on from Key Stage 2 to 3 using, for example, the *European Language Portfolio* (see Chapter 3); in others there is no transfer of information at all. In some schools, e.g. 9–13 middle schools, there is a seamless learning process between Years 6 and 7, although the potential learning gap may still exist above or below this age, as children transfer in this system, for example from 'first' schools at age 9 and to 'high schools' or 'upper schools' at age 13. This illustrates that a school break can weaken the communications structure at any age.

Reception pupils learn languages on the 'magic carpet'

Many children are already exposed to foreign languages outside the school situation through travel; they may be bilingual; they may have a different language as a mother tongue. Providing support for mother-tongue community languages is important in both primary and secondary schools. CILT Young Pathfinder 10: *A world of languages* (Datta and Pomphrey 2004) shows how teachers can encourage children to develop a love of languages by celebrating multiculturalism and multilingualism in the classroom.

With the current diversity of provision for primary languages there is almost inevitably a wide range of attainment by the end of Year 6. There has been criticism that some children do not make real progress in language learning in Key Stage 2, due to the focus on an accumulation of nouns rather than on moving from word to sentence to text level (Martin 2000). Similarly, in Key Stage 3, many children with prior language learning do not make the 'value-added' progress of which they are capable.

 ## PREPARING FOR THE FUTURE

The mixed levels of language knowledge and skills in primary languages among both teachers and children mean that there is an increasing need across the country for primary and secondary teachers to co-operate and to establish a broad consensus of ways to ensure continuity and progression in language. As entitlement by 2010 to language learning in Key Stage 2 approaches, the need for improved communication will become more acute.

A seamless progression from primary puppets to a secondary target-language discussion

1. Getting together

In order to ensure children's continuity of learning when they transfer to secondary schools, there should be effective planning at an early stage, involving primary and secondary schools. Schools need to develop a co-ordinated programme with shared perspectives and transfer of information, e.g. use of a record of achievement or portfolio. Transfer records should make reference to children's progress in the four skill areas of listening, speaking, reading and writing ...

(Modern Foreign Languages: A scheme of work for Key Stage 2 – Teacher's guide (QCA 2000b))

The key to effective transition in MFL is co-operation: teachers and key players getting together early in Key Stage 2 to meet, to talk and to listen, planning together and taking into account the whole-school context.

THE BENEFITS OF CO-OPERATION

Primary teachers need to consider the consequences for secondary teachers when they introduce languages: the choice of language, length of study time, methodology and focus all have impact on the pupils' experience and motivation in Key Stage 3. **Secondary teachers** need to understand that introducing children to a foreign language is no longer their prerogative: there is no more a tabula rasa. They should see this not as a problem but as an advantage, as the pupils with experience of learning languages in the primary school tend to be highly motivated and have already developed a positive attitude to language learning which can be transmitted to other pupils (Gregory 2001). It is the main challenge of the *National Languages Strategy* (DfES 2002), and the aim of this book, to encourage teachers to work together to maintain this motivation in Key Stage 3 and to build on it.

The sheer number of primary schools in England mean that it is unlikely that the teaching of languages can be covered in Years 3–6 through input by secondary or Specialist Language College staff alone. Although these visiting teachers have an important role to play as teachers, role models and trainers in the early years of the national development of primary languages, it will eventually be necessary to train large numbers of generalist primary teachers themselves to deliver the languages programme, as in Scotland (Low 1995). Driscoll (1999) argues that the generalist primary teacher, with some training in the language and in basic foreign-language teaching methodology, is better equipped than a secondary specialist to deliver primary languages, as he or she will automatically search for innovative ways to reinforce the foreign language. The primary teacher will also be able to integrate the language into other lessons and activities. Particularly in this current period building up towards the national entitlement to primary languages, all those with relevant skills and experience can play an important role: primary teachers, secondary colleagues, native speakers, Foreign Language Assistants, classroom assistants, parents and other adults with a language skill. With such a diverse teaching force, communication between the primary and secondary phases is even more crucial. On the following page we consider their possible contributions.

SECONDARY SCHOOLS CAN CONTRIBUTE:

- language improvement and language-teaching methodology to support primary colleagues
- knowledge and experience of the MFL curriculum beyond KS2
- experience of working with children from the age of 11, building on prior learning and experience
- help with developing all four skills
- help with planning for linguistic progression
- MFL assessment skills
- potential access to good facilities and resources
- opportunities for liaison and networking locally
- experience in organising foreign links and visits

PRIMARY SCHOOLS CAN OFFER:

- appropriate methodology: primary colleagues are specialist teachers of children aged 3–11
- knowledge of the curriculum in Foundation, KS1, KS2
- knowledge of the skills children have previously acquired and ways to build on them
- access to resources which can support learning across the curriculum
- links between the foreign language and other curriculum areas
- knowledge of the *National Literacy Strategy*
- the opportunity to use spare moments creatively to develop understanding within the school day to exploit MFL opportunities
- excellent display skills

THE KEY PLAYERS

Whether primary languages are already established or a school is introducing a language for the first time, it is important to value the contributions of all those who will have some influence on the pupils as they move through primary school into secondary school and beyond. Language learning is a skill that has to be built up over a long period of time and, if pupils' progression and continuity of experience are the central concerns, the most important people in the teaching process will need to meet and share expertise. These key people are the **primary and secondary teachers** who teach the foreign language(s) and their **pupils** as they progress through the education system, but the wider group may include:

- **people in regular contact with pupils in school:** parents; Heads of Year; primary Headteachers;
- **local and cluster support**: advisers; Advanced Skills Teachers (ASTs); primary language co-ordinators; adult education and family learning groups; Foreign Language Assistants; foreign teachers and staff from exchanges or links abroad; other native speakers;
- **local policy makers and managers**: school governors; LEAs (especially Pathfinder LEAs) and their representatives;

- **other potential sources of local support**: Specialist Language Colleges; local Comenius centres; potential sponsors and supporters, e.g. trainers – initial teacher training and continuing professional development providers; trainee teachers – from both UK and foreign institutions; university, higher education and further education MFL departments;
- **regional and national support groups**: Early Language Learning Regional Support Groups; Early Language Learning Regional Consultative Groups; British Council Education and Training Group; national bodies (e.g. QCA, DfES, TDA, CILT), embassies and cultural agencies (e.g. Goethe-Institut, Alliance Française, Italian Embassy, Spanish Embassy, Japan Foundation, etc).

People are important. At preliminary meetings to discuss the introduction of primary languages, to consider a joint scheme of work, or to improve liaison between KS2 and KS3 in languages, there should be representatives of all the key groups involved, including classroom teachers, and not only the decision-makers. In all cases, some representation of teachers from both primary and secondary sectors will help to develop better liaison and reduce perceived differences. Clearly not all the people listed above will be able to meet, but there may be opportunities to involve many of them at different times. In the first instance, representatives of the secondary school and group of feeder primary schools or clusters of schools might be appropriate, as well as the members of staff responsible for liaison within a school. These might be a Headteacher, a primary liaison person, the Head of Year 7, the Head of Department or the primary MFL co-ordinator. Collaboration may be limited to a small number of schools, e.g. in a rural area, or may have a particular identity, e.g. church-aided schools in a wider geographical area.

 ## THE PUPILS' PERSPECTIVE – MOTIVATION AND ATTITUDES

In order to involve pupils in the language-learning process, their opinions and feelings need to be taken into account. According to the *NACELL best practice guide* (CILT 2003), children in Richmond on Thames entering Year 7 with an experience of primary languages were:

- *keen, motivated and secure;*
- *less inhibited in using the target language, boys particularly so;*
- *better at listening;*
- *more aware about language;*
- *well versed in pair- and group-work techniques.*

Pupils need to feel comfortable in the next Key Stage. They are often very anxious in Year 7 about going to the 'big school'. They have mixed emotions and attendant fears about making new friends, coping with a bigger building, meeting new members of staff and so on. A secondary teacher who had taught French in the local primary schools tells how the Year 7 pupils would rush towards her, in corridors and playgrounds, to greet her with *'Bonjour Madame!'* and would eagerly answer the question *'Ça va?'*. Sometimes it would take her the whole of break time to reach the staff room! The pupils obviously felt reassured by the presence of a familiar member of staff.

Pupils are also strongly influenced by their siblings and peers. Those with older brothers and sisters or local friends in the 'new school' will often find it easier to settle down, and they will hear about the new teachers and language lessons from them. One way to make settling down easier is to involve large groups of children from different schools in joint activities before they start secondary school (see Chapters 3 and 4).

The pupil needs to be put at the centre of the picture, as his or her experiences in different contexts in and out of school should be taken into account:

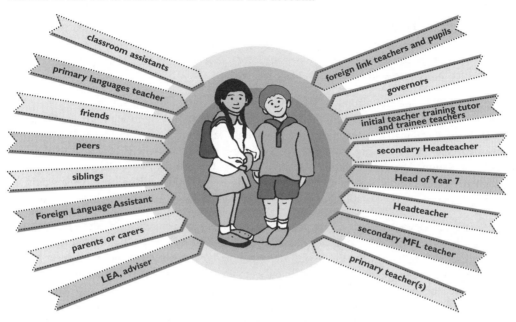

All of the above people have an influence on a child's language-learning experience and on his or her attitudes towards this. In a child's early life, parents or carers have an important influence on attitudes. For example, a child growing up in a bilingual home or in a family which travels abroad is likely to have positive attitudes to language learning, even before starting school. Similarly, a child with a sibling or friend who enjoys learning a language at school will be influenced by his or her experience. In school, a child's attitude towards language learning, and therefore motivation, will be affected by the teacher's enthusiasm, the ethos of the school, the sense of direction and well-being created by the staff, and indirectly by governors, education advisers and teacher trainers. Children are very perceptive and often become de-motivated if they realise that they are repeating in secondary school things they have learnt in primary school. If positive attitudes are developed, motivation increases (Gardner and Lambert 1985).

Research into pupil motivation in languages, covering pupils in primary school who were tracked through into Year 7, shows how many people influence pupil motivation and attitude (Gregory 1996). The comments of pupils, parents and teachers in both phases reflect these influences:

- *'You can usually tell the primary French pupils: they'll answer more quickly, their faces light up with recognition'* (secondary teacher)
- *'They started off with a keen interest, they maintained that interest and they have a high level of success'* (secondary teacher)
- *'They aren't reticent to try the new sounds'* (primary teacher)
- *'The lively approach at [primary] school has opened up an awareness of language. They listen more carefully'* (parent)
- *'My primary French has helped me a lot'* (pupil)
- *'Attitudes are the key'* (secondary teacher)

Singleton (1989) and Johnstone (1994) both agree that when children start to learn a foreign language before the age of eleven, their attitudes towards continuing to learn the language, the speakers of that language, the countries where that language is spoken and indeed learning another foreign language, are more positive than those of children who experience first foreign-language learning later. The children's positive attitudes towards the foreign language and people is enhanced and in adolescence they are more inclined to retain positive attitudes towards the language, the speakers of that language and to language learning in general (Gregory 2001).

For the pupil, language learning is not just about 'lily pads' of separate lists of nouns (see diagram on page 9) – as one pupil in Scotland (quoted by Daniel Tierney) put it, 'I know ten fruits!'. It is far more useful to know what to do with these nouns; how to put them into sentences; how to progress in the language from words to sentences to text. This can be shown diagrammatically as a helix (see below) where the child starts with a little language then moves outwards and upwards, increasing both vocabulary and structures, striving for independence and fluency. Every so often, the teacher will lead the pupil back down the spiral to pick up something that has been forgotten or overlooked before moving up and out again. In short, the language-learning process is a cohesive body of both knowledge and skills (a 'helix'), transferable from one language to another, rather than a series of isolated units ('lily pads') to be memorised.

The task of teachers in both primary and secondary phases is to ensure that the helix of language learning is a continuum, seamlessly growing with the pupil. Communication between phases is therefore crucial. In order to build on pupils' existing knowledge and skills teachers need to know what and how their pupils have learnt. They can then progress, keeping motivation high, especially among 'gifted-and-talented' pupils, with the help of differentiation and by using the foreign language in new contexts.

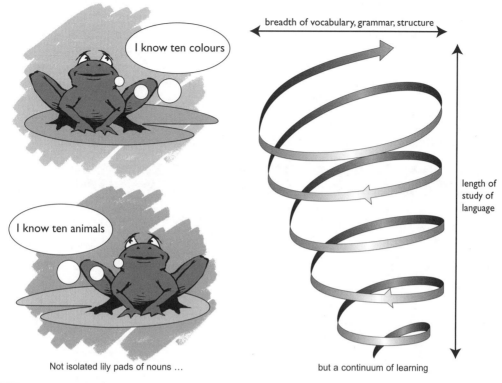

I know ten colours

breadth of vocabulary, grammar, structure

I know ten animals

length of study of language

Not isolated lily pads of nouns ...

but a continuum of learning

COMMUNICATION

If developing and maintaining positive pupil attitudes to languages is one of the keys to success, developing and maintaining effective communication is another. Liaison meetings should establish a basis of mutual trust and help to identify the needs of the pupils and staff of each sector, and enable the teachers to move to a common approach, a shared scheme of work (see below) or to set up a collaborative event which serves the needs of all partners (see Chapters 3 and 4). The process can be started by a simple phone call from the primary teacher to the Head of Languages at the local secondary school.

Having considered all the possible people who may have an impact on pupils learning languages, clear communication strategies should be adopted, to include: regular meetings of the key players (at least once a term, if possible), e-mail links, automatic copying of information such as dates of relevant events in each sector and invitations to representatives from the other sector to these. It is only by meeting the 'other side' that teachers can begin to work together to the child's benefit. Once a person is known by a face rather than just by a name or e-mail address, real collaboration can begin. The first meetings may be formal or informal, reciprocal visits to the different schools, which bring the benefit of putting the faces into a context. Later visits may include observation visits to each other's classrooms, possibly with a short teaching input or observation of a literacy session in the primary school. This allows secondary colleagues to share the vibrant cross-curricular context of the primary classroom and primary teachers to see their former pupils' progress in languages. This is not so much a case of 'seeing is believing' as 'seeing is sharing'. In Richmond upon Thames, where primary languages are well established, at least annual reciprocal observation visits with discussions, wider-scale meetings co-ordinated by the LEA MFL Adviser and cross-phase conferences are carried out at least once a year (quoted in the *NACELL best practice guide*: **www.nacell.org.uk/bestpractice/transit.htm**). The Inspection and Advisory Team says, 'The desirability of fostering links with secondary colleagues cannot be emphasised too strongly'.

Here is an excerpt from the Richmond upon Thames action plan for a school cluster:

Action	By when	Success criteria
Encourage visits to French and German lessons by Y5 pupils	[Secondary teacher] to incorporate this as part of liaison programme and contact schools by end of term	Visits made and become part of usual liaison programme
Exchange of Y6 and Y7 schemes of work	Immediately	Schemes of work passed on and discussed by Y6 teams and MFL dept
Primary teachers to visit Y7 French and Y8 German lessons	Autumn term	Visits completed and feedback given to colleagues
Pupils' portfolios to be shared with French teachers and displayed in MFL area. Portfolios to be returned to pupils	First 2 weeks of Autumn term	Displays to celebrate pupils' language-learning achievements are in place
[Secondary teacher] to primary schools	Tuesday afternoons in Summer term are available	Secondary teachers have met the children and some joint activities have been planned

NACELL best practice guide (CILT 2003)

Whatever the form of meetings, there should be a way of reporting back, for example to secondary departmental and Heads of Department meetings and primary school staff meetings, as well as a record being kept for the LEA and OFSTED. Similarly, there is a need to report back down the line to the teachers, so that any OFSTED comments about primary languages are passed on (in either direction), together with comments by LEA representatives, visitors, etc.

Use of the Internet and intranet for shared websites can also aid communication between institutions, as can e-mail links between both phases and between pupils both primary to primary and also between primary and secondary. Examples of bridging unit links between primary and secondary pupils are given in Chapter 4.

Pupil in La Réunion using the Internet at home

Mutual understanding

Secondary teachers need to understand the skills which are acquired in primary languages such as listening, the ability to concentrate and learning how to learn. They will perhaps be surprised to see how much things have changed since their own primary days, how much rigorous planning is done by the teacher and how he or she has to be skilled and knowledgeable in so many subject areas. Watching skilled generalist primary teachers at work first hand often makes a secondary teacher appreciate their expertise and later re-consider perceived criticism about lack of linguistic accuracy. Primary teachers will also perhaps be surprised by the pace and focus in secondary languages lessons, how the teacher fits so much language into a lesson, the planned use of the 'target language', i.e. using French as much as possible during the French lesson, for example in classroom commands, management and praise (see Young Pathfinder 4: *Keep talking*, Satchwell 1997), and the need to stimulate and motivate some of the pupils, particularly the boys. But both primary and secondary teachers will gain a better understanding of the continuum of learning through these reciprocal visits. If it is possible, they should be planned as a regular part of collaboration and should include teaching a lesson in the other sector. If this is not possible, a joint project or bridging unit can help to achieve the same level of mutual understanding and respect, as well as potentially providing in-service training for both phases (see Chapters 4 and 5).

Dispelling myths and sharing strengths

Although in the past there has sadly been a lack of understanding by both primary and secondary teachers of the demands of and skills required by teaching in the other phase, the closer collaboration and liaison proposed above should help to dispel myths and encourage sharing of strengths. There has previously been a feeling by some primary teachers that secondary teachers ignore what has been achieved by the primary school, take no note of any information that has been passed on, fail to recognise their skills and contribution to the pupils' learning and do not differentiate teaching sufficiently to support, for example, pupils with special educational needs. Some secondary teachers have been heard to criticise primary teachers' poor pronunciation, lack of grammatical accuracy and limited vocabulary, and have failed to notice the pupils' positive attitudes to languages, their ability to understand grammatical structures or their autonomy. Secondary teachers visiting primary schools are often amazed by the generalist knowledge and skills of their primary colleagues, as well as the multi-tasking and differentiation that goes on in the primary classroom. Primary teachers visiting secondary colleagues' language classes admire the depth of subject knowledge, the wide range of language activities planned and the planning for assessment, continuity and progression. It may be true that some primary teachers need linguistic support, as many of those teaching primary languages have not had specialist training or may not be fluent linguists. Secondary teachers of languages are generally specialist graduates and they usually teach only one or two subjects, so have more experience and skills in this area. But they may not be experienced in differentiating their teaching to include children with a particular special need; they may have a limited repertoire of activities which link languages to other subject areas or themes and some may not be as IT-literate as their primary colleagues. Through the meetings and shared visits described above, teachers from both sectors will build up a better understanding of each other's strengths and mutual trust and confidence in each other, so that these issues can be aired and a solution found.

In the absence of support from Pathfinder projects, Specialist Language College, LEA or Advanced Skills Teachers, even small clusters of schools can work together to provide mutual support, whether it is focused on linguistic or pedagogical issues. As a colleague in the East Riding of Yorkshire said, 'Once we knew each other as people, we began to trust each other and then to phone each other, sometimes even just to check how to pronounce a word!'

 ## SUPPORT THROUGH TRAINING

Establishing mutual trust, as identified above, is also important in training courses. Such support is increasingly available, the question is knowing where to look. There are many opportunities for teachers to undertake specific training for teaching primary languages, as well as 'refresher' courses in the chosen language, at universities, colleges and other training institutions.

Many primary teachers require a course in language teaching and methodology, and are often then able to bring their primary pedagogy into play, with lots of creative ideas to reinforce the language in everyday classroom activities.

CILT, the National Centre for Languages holds a **Primary Languages Show** every year and runs successful and stimulating **courses abroad** for primary teachers, with funding available, where linguistic and pedagogical skills are developed. Many primary teachers have a dormant qualification or skill in a foreign language and just need to improve their self-confidence. Participants on the CILT TRAFIC residential course in France, organised for English primary teachers, appreciated the increasing self-confidence that they gained and the way in which their existing skills were valued, as well as the level of trust developed within the group:

> *... courses work best when an atmosphere of trust is created both within the group and between participants and trainers.*

(**www.cilt.org.uk/trafic**)

Support can also be found at the regional **Comenius centres**, which are co-ordinated through CILT and provide a resource centre for languages as well as training and information about languages at all phases, supporting the delivery of the *National Languages Strategy* in a variety of ways. Details of the Comenius Network and its activities can be found at **www.cilt.org.uk/comenius**.

Free in-service training sessions, also co-ordinated by CILT, can be found at the **Early Language Learning Regional Support Groups**. These sessions are run five times a year, usually at the end of the afternoon or early evening. The Regional Support Groups welcome anyone with an interest in primary languages and offer a network of support in many centres across the country. They also provide a focus for discussion if both primary and secondary colleagues attend. Often, visiting experts are invited to discuss a particular aspect of methodology, to present new resources or to describe a project. The meetings provide an opportunity for teachers to find out about local and national events, to look at resources and, most importantly, to meet others who share the same interest and to swap experiences and information. Further details about Regional Support Groups and other professional development, accredited courses and conferences to support primary language teaching, can be found on the NACELL website (**www.nacell.org.uk/regional**).

CILT has produced an invaluable *Early language learning DVD* (previously available on video). It presents examples of primary language teaching in different situations and provides a useful focus for in-service training sessions and curriculum or departmental meetings. It also provides a sound basis for discussion between primary and secondary teachers, showing excellent practice by primary teachers.

The CILT series of *Young Pathfinder* books makes a useful resource library of all aspects of early language learning for schools beginning primary languages (see **www.cilt.org.uk/publications**).

 REFLECTION

This chapter has made the case for meetings between primary teachers who are teaching or have taught the children and secondary teachers who will teach the same children at a later stage in their education. The next chapter suggests how these teachers can plan together their pupils' experiences of language learning.

2. Planning together for continuity and progression

The previous chapter identified the key players involved in transition and encouraged them to meet and communicate effectively in order to put the pupil at the centre and to create mutual understanding, thereby improving language learning in their classrooms. This chapter looks at planning, responds to the common questions surrounding continuity and progression and gives an overview of the supporting documentation available.

 ## FIRST STEPS

Once a decision has been made to introduce primary languages, the task of the key players is to address the following issues in order to ensure continuity from class to class:

- *linguistic progression;*
- *the sustainability of language teaching throughout the school;*
- *the provision of staff;*
- *the provision of resources;*
- *in-service training and staff development, including language refresher courses;*
- *collaboration with secondary schools.*

(**www.nacell.org.uk/bestpractice/transit.htm**)

If there is to be continuity in foreign-language experience, primary schools will need to allocate the responsibility of a **languages co-ordinator or subject leader** to a member of staff and also consider the appointment of new members of staff in this light (see *Piece by piece: Languages in primary schools*, DfES/CILT, distributed to all primary Headteachers in 2004).

In Gloucestershire, primary schools appoint a languages co-ordinator to ensure that the school's aims, policy and scheme of work are compiled and to undertake liaison work with partner primary and secondary schools:

> *French is such an important part of the learning experience for each class that, when recruiting new staff, the school must seriously consider candidates' experience and competence in a foreign language.*

(Barrs Court Primary School, *NACELL best practice guide*)

Once a co-ordinator has been appointed, there are several questions to be answered, e.g. which language? for what purpose?

WHICH LANGUAGE?

Before drawing up a scheme of work the question of which language to teach must first be considered. This may involve an audit of primary teachers' linguistic skills, discussions with the secondary colleagues to ensure continuity and progression and consideration of the bigger picture in a geographical area or LEA.

Since publication of the Primary National Strategy, *Excellence and enjoyment* (DfES 2003a) and *Key Stage 2 Framework for Languages* (DfES 2005), more schools will be seeking a solution to entitlement that is coherent across a cluster or region. The decision about the language taught may be influenced by other schools, but sometimes an individual primary school has a particular aim in introducing a different foreign language to its neighbours, e.g. when there is a foreign link or exchange involved or when a member of staff has a particular expertise. Even in LEAs which support a particular choice of language, such as Nottingham, not all primary schools in the LEA teach the same language and the secondary schools are faced with a diverse intake in Year 7.

In Scotland, where a diversification in the choice of foreign language was encouraged during the early days of the Modern Languages in the Primary School scheme, there has been some regression from this diversity to a situation where schools have changed from Spanish, German or Italian to French. As a result of staff skills and secondary timetable issues, more teachers are available to teach French than other languages, and in small schools if, for example, the sole Italian teacher left the school, a replacement could not always be found to ensure a continuity of language (Tierney and De Cecco 1999; Martin 2000). However, the bilingual approach to primary languages in Wales, the success of the Gaelic-medium project in Scotland and the diversification of languages in Irish schools (Harris 2002), together with the diversity of provision in Pathfinder LEAs, suggest that there is no 'best' solution to the question 'Which language?'. The important thing is to involve all the key players in the decision and evaluate, review and modify the model as appropriate.

FOR WHAT PURPOSE?

The *Key Stage 2 Framework for Languages* gives a clear focus to language teaching, with an emphasis on developing speaking and listening skills in the early stages, and on developing reading and writing skills as children become familiar with accurate pronunciation. The issues of developing children's intercultural understanding and knowledge about language are also included in the *Framework*, and schools need to produce schemes of work which address these aims; this is discussed later in the chapter. The primary strategy *Excellence and enjoyment* (DfES 2003a) promotes the possibilities for languages to add to a broad primary curriculum and to contribute towards creativity. It also encourages schools to work together, rather than in isolation. *Excellence and enjoyment* suggests ways in which languages can be embedded in other subjects, creating a more stimulating context for learning. It focuses on the individual and on building on previous knowledge and skills, and encourages assessment for learning, suggesting strategies to improve the transfer and transition situations. These issues will be considered in Chapter 3.

Pupils enjoy performing, e.g. in an assembly

To ensure continuity, one language will usually be taught through Key Stage 2, but some individual schools may also choose to introduce 'tasters' of more than one language, linking language work with the *National Literacy Strategy* (see Young Pathfinder 9: *The literacy link*, Cheater and Farren 2001); or they may focus on an intercultural aim or teach a mother-tongue community language to all pupils; others may decide to teach the two languages taught in the secondary school to reflect future options. Provided the aim is clear, well articulated and is recognised by teachers in the secondary phase there isn't yet any legal requirement to teach a particular language for a particular length of time in a particular way, although there is an expectation in the *National Languages Strategy* that children will reach approximately Level 4 if they have had an entitlement from Year 3. This might influence the decision about the choice of language to be followed, as taster courses are unlikely to afford this level of achievement.

It is hoped that the *Key Stage 2 Framework* will in due course link systematically with the *Key Stage 3 Framework* (DfES 2003b) and with learning beyond secondary school, as is shown in the diagram below:

A new paradigm for languages

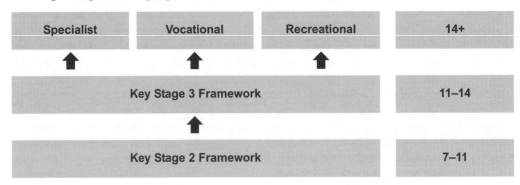

The new Languages Ladder recognition scheme (see Chapter 3) will further strengthen continuity through pupil assessment.

FAMILIARITY OF CONTEXT

Apart from establishing an agreed language base, a familiar approach to cross-curricular links and a shared link with a foreign partner or area, a common methodology can reassure pupils as they transfer from one school to another. By choosing a known game or song, using a familiar poster or resource, a known website or computer programme and displaying work they have started in the primary school, the secondary teacher can immediately show the class that there are effective communication systems between schools. Of course, it is practically impossible for secondary teachers to pick up and use all the potential links with every feeder primary school. It is equally impossible, as well as inappropriate, to dictate that every feeder school should teach primary languages in exactly the same way, using the same materials and list of vocabulary. It is, however, valuable for pupils to see that their teachers in different Key Stages have obviously met and spoken to each other, have a similar approach to teaching languages and know what has gone before. In Chapter 6 we will look at practical activities which will support mixed pupil experiences.

CONTINUITY OF SIMPLE LANGUAGE

Even the old favourite 'Head, shoulders, knees and toes' can provide a link from primary to secondary language learning

When planning the scheme of work, it is important to establish the phrases used for classroom instructions and to ensure that all teachers, whether primary or secondary, are aware of these. Pupils can easily become anxious if a new teacher uses a phrase which is slightly different from the one they are used to (e.g. '*levez le doigt*' instead of '*levez la main*'). In the first encounters between secondary teacher and pupils it is therefore important, for the sake of continuity, to use the known phrases and to gradually introduce variety later on.

Even ensuring that children are confident in the correct pronunciation/knowledge of numbers and alphabet can provide a solid foundation for further work in subsequent years. For example, in Key Stage 1 or in Years 3 and 4 of Key Stage 2, pupils should be able to count confidently to twenty, do simple sums and know the foreign alphabet, so that they can, for example, spell out their names and recognise sound/spelling links. This knowledge can be built into many activities throughout Key Stages 1 and 2, and numbers and letters of the alphabet can be reinforced easily by the class teacher so that the foreign language is used naturally to participate in any activity involving numbers and letters. Consequently in Key Stage 3, pupils should be able to spell words aloud, e.g. names in telephone conversations, and use numbers confidently, without counting on their fingers. Secondary teachers, who have less time to spend on reinforcement of basic skills and knowledge, will appreciate this and will be able to spend more time on developing new skills and knowledge.

CROSS-CURRICULAR LINKS

Languages can be linked with most other areas of the curriculum (see QCA *Key Stage 2 MFL scheme of work* 2000a) and these links need to be explicit in the scheme of work. The Primary National Strategy, *Excellence and enjoyment* (DfES 2003a) encourages teachers to develop a holistic approach to learning, making links between different learning experiences and putting learning into a meaningful context.

The *NACELL best practice guide* provides detailed planning sheets and a curriculum map for planning the Year 3 curriculum. For example there, is a link from language to number patterns in Maths, to using adjectives in English and to cultural songs in Music. Further examples of cross-curricular links can be found in Chapter 3, and also in Young Pathfinder 7: *Making the link* (Tierney and Hope 1998) and in the *Key Stage 2 Framework for Languages*.

Teachers in the secondary phase can build on cross-curricular links and, once again, familiarity with an approach can help to motivate pupils and to reassure them in the next Key Stage. Numeracy, Literacy, Geography, Music and PE are all subjects where the language can very easily be used to reinforce the knowledge and skills taught in the discrete language lesson. There are specific examples of these cross-curricular links in the QCA *Scheme of work* and the *Key Stage 2 Framework for Languages*.

> *Planning for progression and integration into other curricular areas … Effective integration will enable a coherent learning route to be planned, which takes account of the relevant progression in MFL and makes connections to knowledge, skills and understanding in other subjects.*

> (International Learning and Research Centre, South Gloucestershire, *NACELL best practice guide*)

In situations where cross-curricular links are made, a foreign language becomes a means of authentic communication rather than simply a subject in isolation. Pupils tend to focus, for example, on their singing or physical activity, rather than being concerned about getting the right pronunciation, and they pick up phrases and sound patterns in a stress-free way. When the foreign language is linked to numeracy, even if the linguistic content is limited (for example, to numbers), it is still possible to challenge the pupils mathematically (see examples in Chapter 4). Similarly, in linking language to Geography, the geographical knowledge can be reinforced at an appropriate level and can provide an opportunity to use 'real language for real purposes'.

One of the advantages of a primary teacher delivering the foreign language is that he or she can slip into the foreign language at any point of the day or week and, using known or new language, can recap or reinforce another subject area. Secondary teachers rarely have this opportunity to link languages ad hoc with other areas that their pupils are learning. In some schools, however, other subjects are taught through the medium of the foreign language, as for example in Aberdeen (Johnstone 2003) and in the well-documented immersion school situation in Canada, where primary pupils are taught in French (Hammerley 1989). The CILT Content and Language Integration Project (CLIP, 2004) worked in eight secondary schools to teach other subject areas through the medium of the foreign language, using an integrated approach (**www.cilt.org.uk/clip**).

If teachers do make cross-curricular links, they often find that pupil motivation increases. This is due to pupils' perceptions that they are learning a language for a purpose. It also illustrates the enrichment that can come from establishing links with foreign schools and pupils.

Display of cross-curricular work in French, based on La Réunion

FOREIGN LINKS AND EXCHANGES

Any link with a foreign school and its pupils is motivating for those involved, but it can also provide an opportunity for secondary teachers to build on previous experiences. In some clusters of schools it may be possible, in the secondary school, to follow up foreign trips, visits and exchanges made by primary teachers with an exchange link to a school in the same area. Some LEAs have specific links with partner areas abroad and secondary pupils can return to towns they visited earlier as primary pupils. Primary pupils may be accommodated in hostels or study centres, rather than with families, but personal contacts can be strengthened through e-mail links and exchange of text messages, pupil work and videoconferencing links. Even sixth-form work-experience links may be made to the same places, thus creating a lasting partnership with a foreign environment and a real purpose for language learning. Addressing progression and transition through existing links with a school abroad, using links with primary schools and secondary schools in same area can be very beneficial.

The organisation and planning of a trip abroad is very demanding on staff, but brings great rewards. Some schools manage to take pupils in Year 6 to France, or to other countries, before transfer to secondary. Some do so as part of a cluster visit. Judy Hawker wrote about a primary/secondary visit to St Omer on the ell-forum:

> *I was part of a primary/secondary day visit to St Omer. The visit was organised by Patcham High School in Brighton … more details can be obtained form the Head of Department. It was an excellent visit. I took pupils from Year 6/7 from the special school where I teach MFL. We are part of Patcham High Cluster alongside other primary schools, whose pupils also went to St Omer. Over 100 pupils were involved including about half of Year 7 at Patcham High.*

In the Wythenshawe Education Action Zones, Manchester, primary and secondary pupils have worked together on several language projects involving trips abroad. In 2003–2004, pupils from Years 5, 6 and 7 worked on *Shakespeare per i ragazzi*, taking twelve plays including one about the Montagues and Capulets to Bologna, where they also met their Italian penpals and had a chance to test out their language skills. One parent said, 'Thank you for the opportunity you have given our son … we are very proud of him and we are sure he will never forget the experience'. One of the pupils said, 'All the hard work was really worth it and I have made lots of new friends'. The pupils also performed the play in front of a large audience of parents and teachers in St John Fisher and Thomas More Primary School in Wythenshawe. *Shakespeare per i ragazzi* won a European Award for Languages in 2004.

© *Shakespeare per i ragazzi* project

DEVELOPING A SHARED SCHEME OF WORK

One of the key documents for any teacher is a scheme of work with clear, relevant aims and objectives. Once the decision has been made about which language, or languages, will be taught, the scheme of work in Key Stage 2 can be written. This should be made available to all teachers in the primary school and also to the secondary teachers who receive their pupils, in order to assist with continuity and progression. The issues of developing children's intercultural understanding and knowledge about language are also included in the *Key Stage 2 Framework* and schools need to produce schemes of work which address these aims.

The *Key Stage 2 MFL Schemes of work*, published by QCA (2000a) *enables teachers to guide children's progression in:*

- *developing language skills and language-learning skills;*
- *listening, speaking, reading and writing skills;*
- *awareness of different countries, cultures and people;*
- *developing understanding of how language works;*
- *understanding, learning and applying some aspects of grammar.*

Pupils can 'use previously learnt vocabulary and structures in new contexts, e.g. substitute different nouns/verbs/structures in a range of different topics.' They can 'develop intercultural understanding by establishing contact with a partner school abroad, and then using the Internet to compare and contrast language and culture' *(QCA Teacher's guide* 2000b*).*

These schemes of work can be customised to suit the needs of individual schools, clusters of schools or whole LEAs; they provide a scheme of work for Years 5 and 6, with twelve units of study in French, German and Spanish (and the Learning Objectives have been linked to the *Schemes of work,* so that teachers can see how the schemes of work relate to the *Framework*). Many schools currently use the schemes of work over four years instead of two, starting in Year 3 and adapting them slightly so that the early units are suitable for younger children. They are available as a hard copy or may be downloaded from QCA website (**www.qca.org.uk/ca/subjects/mfl/prim_schools.asp**). Other examples of schemes of work can be found in the *NACELL best practice guide* (**www.nacell.org.uk/bestpractice**).

In **South Gloucestershire**, children are taught languages in Key Stage 1 in short 5–10 minute lessons. This is increased in Key Stage 2, so that Year 6 pupils experience 3 x 30 minutes of language learning per week. This build-up of time takes into account the concentration span and needs of younger children as well as their increasing range of language. Young Pathfinder 11: *A flying start* (Satchwell and de Silva 2004) gives useful advice about writing a scheme of work and getting started with primary languages.

As part of the DELL (Development of Early Language Learning) project, teachers in the **City of York** developed a shared scheme of work in French, subsequently translated into Spanish, which was firmly based on the QCA scheme. However, to fit local needs, it was written so that it could be used both in schools with separate Year 5 and Year 6 as well as schools with split Year 5–6 classes, which required a two-year rolling programme. To support the non-specialist teacher, the scheme included detailed reference to key phrases and vocabulary, plans of teaching activities with the necessary vocabulary, and lists of resources, including ideas for ICT and the interactive whiteboard. It was printed so that the teacher could see the detailed lesson plan at a glance.

Key Stage 2 and Key Stage 3 Frameworks

Key Stage 2 Framework for Languages

The *Key Stage 2 Framework for Languages* (DfES 2005) is a core document which offers schools practical support as they plan to introduce languages into the curriculum. It is based on five strands:

- Oracy (listening and speaking);
- Literacy (reading and writing);
- Knowledge about language;
- Intercultural understanding
- Language learning strategies

It is content-free and is designed to help in the planning of a scheme of work in any language, based on a minimum of 60 minutes delivery time per week, embedding languages in the primary curriculum. It shows progression in the four language skills and gives sample activities for the classroom which are suggestions which might help the children to meet the learning objectives. The *Framework* builds on the QCA *Key Stage 2 schemes of work for languages*, which are already used by many schools.

Anticipated progression from Year 3 to Year 6 is clearly shown in the four strands. For example in Oracy, children should be taught to:

Year 3	Year 4	Year 5	Year 6
O.3.1 Listen and respond to simple stories, finger rhymes and songs	O.4.1 Memorise and present a short spoken text	O.5.1 Prepare and practise a simple conversation, reusing familiar vocabulary and structures in new contexts	O.6.1 Understand the main points and simple opinions in a story, song or passage

The *Key Stage 2 Framework* includes sections on:

- Co-ordinating provision: Advice for Headteachers, Senior Managers and Subject Co-ordinators;
- Getting started: Advice for primary schools and teachers introducing languages for the first time;
- Moving on: Advice for primary schools and teachers already teaching languages;
- Supporting primary entitlement: Advice for secondary schools.

Further guidelines are due to be published by the DfES in Spring 2006.

Until primary languages are fully established through Years 3–6, secondary teachers will need to be aware of exactly what pupils entering Year 7 have experienced and can do in the foreign language. The issues surrounding transfer of information and assessment are considered in Chapter 3.

KEY STAGE 3 FRAMEWORK FOR MFL

The *Key Stage 3 Framework for MFL* has been available to secondary schools since 2003 and was written when many Year 7 pupils had not learnt a language in primary school. It currently contains the following objectives:

- Words;
- Sentences;
- Texts: reading and writing;
- Listening and speaking;
- Cultural knowledge and contact.

It aims for progression by providing a firm foundation in Year 7, through promoting acceleration of learning in Year 8 and independence in Year 9. It builds on the *Literacy Strategy*, making concepts and linguistic conventions explicit and encourages interactive learning, the use of ICT and the development of pupil autonomy. The *Key Stage 3 Strategy* will need to be revised in the light of the *Key Stage 2 Framework*. It is important that primary teachers know what is to be covered in the *Key Stage 3 Framework* and that secondary teachers have read the *Key Stage 2 Framework*. For example, pupils entering Year 7 will already be familiar with grammatical terms and with the concept of starters and plenaries, whether or not they have learned a foreign language before Year 7. The comparison between expectations of achievement and methodology in Years 6 and 7 will be a useful basis for discussion when primary and secondary colleagues meet. Chapter 6 suggests appropriate methodology for mixed groups in Year 7.

REFLECTION

This chapter has suggested how primary and secondary teachers can plan together for language teaching, particularly looking at continuity of language and context, cross-curricular links and foreign exchanges, schemes of work and the *Key Stage 2* and *Key Stage 3 MFL Framework* documents. The next chapter will consider how information about pupils' achievement can be recorded and transferred, and will also look at the issue of assessment.

3. Transfer of information and assessment

The previous chapter explored how teachers can plan together for continuity and progression. This chapter deals with the transfer of information about pupils' progress, for example using the *European Language Portfolio*. It then discusses assessment in foreign languages, in particular the Languages Ladder, National Recognition Scheme.

Some primary teachers send their secondary colleagues a summary of their scheme of work with a list of topics covered. They may also send a brief 'report' about each child, so that pupils are not just names on a list. However, until recently some primary teachers have felt that taking time out from limited language teaching time for assessment has not been valuable because many secondary schools, faced with an intake which includes pupils with prior language experience and those without, have 'started from scratch'. Others have not established regular contact with their secondary colleagues and are convinced that they never read the information which is sent to them. On the other hand, some secondary colleagues believe that the assessment of pupils' linguistic skills may be unrealistic or over-generous and that primary teachers are not trained to assess these skills.

Since primary languages entitlement involves teaching pupils for four years, more and more Year 6 pupils will achieve potentially higher and higher levels. Primary and secondary teachers must work together to remove misconceptions and mistrust and to ensure greater collaboration in the assessment process. If there is to be continuity and progression, the secondary teacher needs to know exactly what his or her primary counterpart has been teaching. Furthermore, primary teachers will appreciate receiving information about past pupils as they reach the end of Year 7 and beyond, as this can help them in their approach to the teaching of their current Key Stage 2 pupils.

 ## TRANSFER OF ATTAINMENT INFORMATION

For practical reasons the information transferred to secondary colleagues needs to be relevant, precise, manageable and useful. It may include:

*   a summary or copy of the primary scheme of work;
*   a list of topics which have been covered (so that if primary pupils have, for example, covered zoo animals, secondary colleagues will be able to revise these but introduce domestic animals);
*   the skills developed;
*   a list of key phrases which are familiar to the children;
*   a class list with information about number of years of prior language learning;
*   comments about mother-tongue community language and bilingualism;
*   particular points of interest, e.g. links abroad, penfriends;
*   a note about achievement in each skill, if appropriate.

Below is an example of a very simple planner sheet used by some schools in York to highlight the language areas covered in the primary school. This formed part of a larger document, which gave more detailed information to the secondary school about the pupil's overall progress and achievement. It was later replaced by the *European Language Portfolio* (see page 27).

Modern Languages Planner

Language: ....

Name: ....

Primary school: ....

Term: ....

Topic: ....

I have learnt to:

....

....

Some LEAs are developing a more systematic approach to the transfer of information between Key Stages 2 and 3 and are aware that this information exchange should not be a one-way process. In the future, this exchange of documents should form part of regular communication and the information on prior language experience should be freely available to the Year 7 teachers who will be able to take this into account when planning their teaching. Below is another example of a planner.

NOMBRE: Me llamo ....

What I can say and understand in Spanish

	Yes I can	I can with help	I've forgotten
	✔	✔	✔

FOOD AND DRINK
I can say the names of these things to eat and drink:

juice	☐	☐	☐
water	☐	☐	☐

Source: *Early Start Spanish: Mi ciudad y mi colegio* (Rowe & Kilbery 2002)

Creating an anxiety-free environment

This exchange of information will also help the new Year 7s to feel more at ease. Coping with the practicalities of life at Key Stage 3 can be overwhelming. Among other issues, many children, particularly from small or rural schools, feel totally over-awed by the sheer size of the secondary buildings, especially as they have to move from room to room for different classes. Further examples of differences pupils will encounter in the secondary school are listed in the *Curriculum continuity* document (DfES 2004):

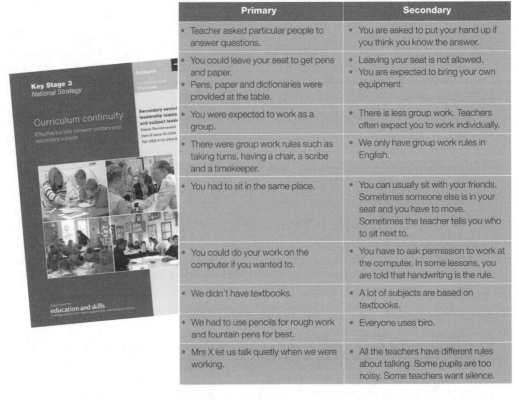

Primary	Secondary
• Teacher asked particular people to answer questions.	• You are asked to put your hand up if you think you know the answer.
• You could leave your seat to get pens and paper. • Pens, paper and dictionaries were provided at the table.	• Leaving your seat is not allowed. • You are expected to bring your own equipment.
• You were expected to work as a group.	• There is less group work. Teachers often expect you to work individually.
• There were group work rules such as taking turns, having a chair, a scribe and a timekeeper.	• We only have group work rules in English.
• You had to sit in the same place.	• You can usually sit with your friends. Sometimes someone else is in your seat and you have to move. Sometimes the teacher tells you who to sit next to.
• You could do your work on the computer if you wanted to.	• You have to ask permission to work at the computer. In some lessons, you are told that handwriting is the rule.
• We didn't have textbooks.	• A lot of subjects are based on textbooks.
• We had to use pencils for rough work and fountain pens for best.	• Everyone uses biro.
• Mrs X let us talk quietly when we were working.	• All the teachers have different rules about talking. Some pupils are too noisy. Some teachers want silence.

Creating an anxiety-free transfer and developing self-esteem and self-confidence among pupils is key to successful transition. Research into pupil attitudes to language learning at the transfer point shows that pupils appreciated the fact that they were not facing a new subject, that they had met the new teacher before they started in Year 7 and that their primary language learning would help them to fit into the secondary school more easily (Gregory 2001).

What we have said about ensuring a smooth transition and a clear transfer of information at the Key Stage 2–3 transfer point equally applies, albeit to a generally lesser degree, at any point of change – the Key Stage 1–2 transition point, or when there is a change of teacher, for whatever reason. The main difference is that when the transfer is to an unfamiliar, larger, more distant building, the transfer of knowledge and information about pupils is more crucial. Once again, the position of the pupil must be considered. Responsibility to provide a bridge of communication at this point does not rest with only one person – it is for all players to be involved and to make sure that information is passed on, that it reaches the right person (and not just before a holiday, particularly the summer break!), is read and acted upon.

EUROPEAN LANGUAGE PORTFOLIO

The *European Language Portfolio* is a useful tool to support assessment. The first page tells the pupil:

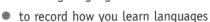

THIS PORTFOLIO IS FOR YOU

- to keep a record of your progress in
  learning languages
- to record how you learn languages

my language
BIOGRAPHY

- to keep some examples of work you've done
  in languages

my language
DOSSIER

- to show which languages you know
- to show what you know and can do in
  languages

my language
PASSPORT

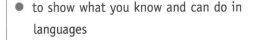

Schools which have used the *European Language Portfolio* have been positive in their feedback. Pupils have enjoyed filling in the bubbles of 'can-do' statements and have particularly enjoyed adding their own work into the 'My Dossier' section, even including videos and audio tapes of their performances. Pupils should update their Portfolios on a regular basis and particularly at the end of Year 6. The *NACELL best practice guide* gives examples of using the Portfolio, illustrating both the motivation of pupils to record their progress and the high levels of attainment. Pupils have been proud to share the content of their Portfolios with visitors. In one York primary school pupils were told that the Portfolios were expensive, so they should take care of them so that they would be able to look back later and see how they had made progress. One boy whispered loudly to his neighbour, 'I'll flog it!', but a girl said that she would want to show it to her grandchildren and have it placed in her coffin!

The ELP is the property of the child and in many schools pupils are encouraged to take this with them when they leave, to show the secondary teachers. Large class sets are too bulky to keep in the classroom, so one solution to these problems might be to use the summary page of the ELP, which could be photocopied and given to the secondary teacher. One teacher in a European school devised a single sheet with the 'can-do' bubble statements spread across the page, so that the simplest were in the middle and the more challenging statements were on the outside (see page 29). The teacher had a sheet for each pupil and the bubbles were coloured in at different times in the year when both the pupil and teacher agreed they were achieved. The following year's sheet had similar bubbles, but the 'simple' targets were concentrated at the centre, allowing space around the outside for new and more challenging statements. By using a different colour at each assessment/check point, the pupil's progress could be roughly measured. In this way, information about each pupil's linguistic ability and progress could be passed on in a simple and manageable form. This idea could be adapted for the Key Stage 2/3 transfer point, using, for example, electronically filled-in copies of the summary document, which could easily be e-mailed to whichever secondary school the pupil transferred to. With the introduction of the Languages Ladder the transfer of validated and useful information from class to class and school to school will become simpler.

It may be possible to arrange a time in Year 7 when pupils can look back at their Portfolios together and update them to reflect their new achievements. The Portfolio can be adapted to suit the needs of a particular school or cluster and a new edition (Spring 2006) will reflect the Languages Ladder; sections of the new guide can be completed, stored and transferred electronically. It may be ordered as a hard copy from CILT or it can be downloaded from **www.nacell.org.uk/elp.htm**.

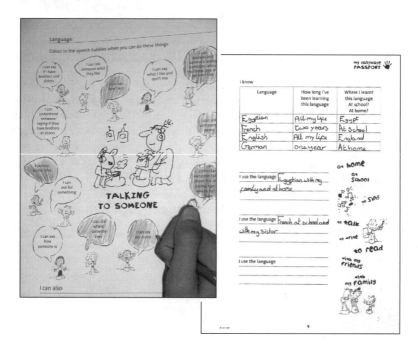

EXAMPLE OF PUPIL PROGRESS IN ENGLISH SHEET

by David Cudworth, European School in Varese, Italy

This simple record was devised so teachers of English at the European School in Varese, Italy, could colour in the squares as they noted that pupils had achieved the different skills. The squares could be shaded in different colours to indicate when the skill was achieved and the skills not covered by the class could be included in the boxes for the next year. Some boxes were left blank so that teachers could add their own items. This grid was devised for classes which incorporated two different year groups – coloured yellow and orange. The teacher was able to focus on a small group of pupils at a time, which made the assessment process both manageable and flexible.

(Y1:Yellow; Y2: Orange) ENGLISH II Language assessment Name of pupil:						
	Can describe what they are wearing	Can name some clothes in English	Can describe the weather in simple terms	Can ask someone their age and say how old they are	Can name some school objects in English	
Can describe what another person is wearing	Can name some colours in English	Can introduce him-/herself and say 'hello' + 'goodbye'	Enjoys singing songs in English	Can ask someone their name	Can name some means of transport in English	Can name some furniture and rooms in the house
Has an awareness of the negative forms in English	Can name a range of animals in English	Can say how he/she comes to school	ENJOYS FIRST STEPS IN ENGLISH	Listens attentively	Repeats accurately	Can describe the location of an object, using 'on', 'in', 'under', etc
Can name some parts of an animal	Can name some toys in English	Can ask and answer simple questions	Has an awareness of the plural form in English	Knows numbers 1–5	Knows numbers 1–10	Can describe own and someone else's appearance
Can use expressions 'I can', 'I can't' accurately	Can describe the size of an object	Grasps the general meaning of stories, songs and rhymes	Volunteers to take an active part in role play	Follows simple instructions carefully	Knows a range of action words in English	Can talk about possessions using 'I've got …'
Can describe daily routines with confidence	Can name some food in English	Understands 'What's your favourite …?' and responds appropriately	Can express likes/dislikes	Uses the expressions 'please' and 'thank you'	Can name parts of the body in English	Knows numbers 1–20
		Can retell a familiar story in English	Knows the days of the week	Is an able and confident speaker who can hold a conversation		

ASSESSMENT FACILITATES TRANSITION

In many schools, primary languages have been regarded as a bonus 'fun' activity, which is taught outside the formal curriculum and without the restraints of formal assessment. Indeed, some teachers have argued that if pupils' achievement were to be tested or evaluated, the 'fun' element would be lost. In the move towards entitlement, as primary languages are increasingly included in the school's timetable, teachers have begun to look more closely at the question of assessment. They are also realising that language teaching can be both fun and have a clear purpose, which gives them another incentive to plan for progression and to find evidence of success These teachers already use informal assessment of pupils' achievement in primary languages formatively, to plan for progression, and many work with pupils to self-assess their work as part of the *European Language Portfolio*.

For secondary teachers, assessment has not been optional, and one of the great strengths of secondary language teachers is their experience in assessing pupils' language learning and planning for linguistic progression. By passing on the knowledge they have gained they can help primary teachers to develop the same skills.

Pupils are keen to know what they have achieved and their motivation increases when they see the progress they have made – assessment helps to give credibility and status to a subject/curriculum area. In the 1970s, Graded Objectives in Modern Foreign Languages were introduced into secondary schools, with a resulting increase in pupil motivation (Buckby 1981). These tests took pupils in small stages over five years towards a CSE or GCE exam and a certificate was awarded at each stage. Nowadays, some primary schools award a certificate to pupils to reflect their achievement in languages, but there is little formal assessment to differentiate levels of achievement. All teachers want to know what their pupils can do and when these pupils move to a different class or school, the new teachers want to know what they have done, to inform future teaching. The question is how to assess, how to record the achievement and how to transfer the information.

Below are examples of the Richmond upon Thames Bravo certificate and the Lingua badge award, which are awarded to pupils at the end of their primary language experience:

PROGRAMMES OF STUDY AND NATIONAL CURRICULUM LEVELS

The National Curriculum levels in the Programmes of Study and non-statutory guidelines are applicable to both primary and secondary pupils. These can be found in full under 'Attainment targets' on the Key Stage 3 MFL section of the website (**www.nc.uk.net**). Although they are not currently used by many primary teachers to describe individual pupils, they provide a useful basis for assessment. Using pair or group assessment, confirmed by the teacher, it is possible to record a level in the relevant skills against a register in a relatively short time, for transfer to the secondary school. It may not be appropriate to record information about all skills, as many schools currently focus on oral skills, but many pupils reach Levels 1–2 in Key Stage 1 and Levels 3–4 by the end of Key Stage 2 in Speaking and Listening and Understanding (see table below). Increasing numbers of pupils are learning to read and write in the foreign language in primary school and secondary teachers need to know their capabilities.

ATTAINMENT TARGET 2: SPEAKING LEVELS 1–3

Level 1	Level 2	Level 3
Pupils respond briefly, with single words or short phrases, to what they see and hear. Their pronunciation may be approximate and they may need considerable support from a spoken model and from visual clues.	Pupils give short, simple responses to what they see and hear. They name and describe people, places and objects. They use set phrases (e.g. to ask for help and permission). Their pronunciation may still be approximate and the delivery hesitant, but their meaning is clear.	Pupils take part in brief prepared tasks of at least two or three exchanges, using visual or other cues to help them initiate and respond. They use short phrases to express personal responses (e.g. likes, dislikes, feelings). Although they use mainly memorised language, they occasionally substitute items of vocabulary to vary question or statements.

COLLABORATIVE ASSESSMENT

Primary Language Days (see Chapters 4 and 5) provide a possible opportunity for collaborative assessment by primary and secondary colleagues, or at least moderation of primary teachers' grading. Secondary colleagues may be able to suggest different techniques and these days also provide an informal opportunity to share information about the pupils as well as providing a real reason for both phases to work together. It may be possible for primary and secondary teachers to 'swap' teaching for half a day or to be released to co-teach in the 'other' school. This gives a valuable opportunity for each to see how the other operates, the different pressures and demands on the teachers and the responses of the pupils. It is also a chance to assess pupils, either formally or informally, in the context of the primary or secondary scheme of work.

THE LANGUAGES LADDER – STEPS TO SUCCESS

The new National Recognition Scheme, the Languages Ladder, launched in Autumn 2005, provides both formal and informal opportunities for teachers to assess the progress of primary language learners against a national scale in the four discrete skills – Listening, Speaking, Reading and Writing (see **www.dfes.gov.uk/languages/languagesladder.cfm**). The Languages Ladder 'can-do' statements can be used for assessment for learning, peer and self-assessment, and provide the core criteria for the 'formalised' teacher-assessment and external tests.

This will assist the transition between Key Stages 2 and 3 by providing secondary teachers with information about each individual pupil's achievement. Teachers will then be able to build on this and provide 'value-added' achievement in Key Stage 3. The testing is intended to be 'just in time', so that pupils can take the assessment when they are ready to do so; the tests are paper-based, with all but the speaking tests also being available on-line. It is anticipated that at the end of Year 6 pupils should be able to achieve at least the first stage of the Ladder (the Breakthrough stage), although they may not choose to be assessed in all four skills.

The National Recognition Scheme reflects the Common European Framework of Reference with the Breakthrough stage, subdivided into three grades, roughly equating to the Common European Framework Level A1 or National Curriculum Levels 1–3:

The Common European Framework of Reference for Languages: Learning, teaching, assessment

Basic user	A1	Can understand and use familiar everyday expressions and very basic phrases aimed at the satisfaction of needs of a concrete type. Can introduce him/herself and others and can ask questions about personal details such as where he/she lives, people he/she knows and things he/she has. Can interact in a simple way provided the other person talks slowly and clearly and is prepared to help.

Source: **www.culture2.coe.int/portfolios/documents_intro/common_framework.html**

The grade descriptors are 'can-do' statements, reflecting the *European Language Portfolio*. The synergy between the Languages Ladder and the *European Language Portfolio* should help both pupils and teachers to see how to make progress to the next stage. The Languages Ladder scheme is voluntary, but teachers and pupils in both Key Stages will welcome the opportunity to produce evidence of their achievement, and pupils' motivation in languages should be enhanced in the same way that national gymnastic or music awards increase motivation in those areas.

Primary teachers will be involved in the assessment within each three stages of the grades but there will be external assessment at the interface between the stages, e.g. between Breakthrough and Preliminary levels. The can-do statements are generic, so applicable to all languages. The task types used in the teacher assessment and external testing are similar across the range of languages. The Languages Ladder tests are skills-based rather than content-based, although there will be a core of key required vocabulary geared to the age of the candidate as the tests are aimed at any language learner, from 'cradle to grave'. There is a discrete set of primary languages tasks covering a specific set of language functions. The Languages Ladder also gives the opportunity to formally recognise mother-tongue community languages in the way that the *European Language Portfolio* has informally done so in the past. Both for pupil motivation and self-esteem, as well as for acknowledgment of achievement in primary languages, the Languages Ladder is an exciting initiative. In addition, it provides a valuable benchmark for transition.

LANGUAGES LADDER

Breakthrough: Grade 3

Listening: I can understand the main point(s) from a short spoken passage	**Speaking**: I can ask and answer simple questions and talk about my interests
Reading: I can understand the main point(s) from a short written text in clear printed script	**Writing**: I can write a few short sentences with support using expressions which I have already learned

Preliminary: Grade 4

Listening: I can understand the main point(s) and some of the detail from a short spoken passage	**Speaking**: I can take part in a simple conversation and I can express my opinions
Reading: I can understand the main point(s) and some of the detail from a short written text	**Writing**: I can write a short text on a familiar topic, adapting language which I have already learned

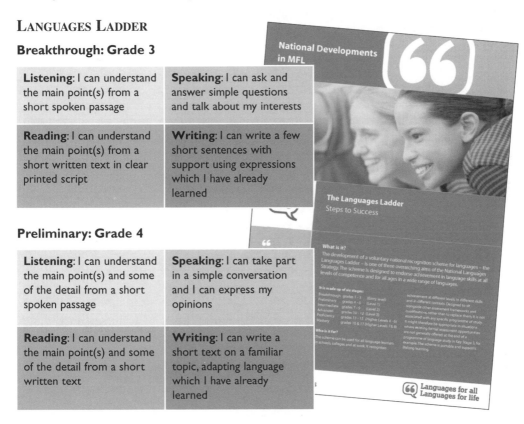

Can-do statements are given above as examples, but the progress should be assessed for each skill individually. If the Languages Ladder is used by primary teachers at the end of Year 6, secondary colleagues will have a much clearer picture than previously of what these pupils can do at the beginning of Year 7. Secondary teachers may also decide to use the Ladder for assessment at the end of Key Stage 3 or at the end of Key Stage 4, as accreditation for an alternative language course. Thus, for the first time both primary and secondary teachers may potentially be using the same system of assessment, providing a framework for a continuum of learning. Pupils and parents will also know where they are on the scale and what they must achieve to reach the next level. This transparency will inform planning and teaching of languages in both phases and put the pupil at the centre of the discussions. Information about the Languages Ladder can be ordered from DfES Publications (Prolog), tel: 0845 602 2260 (can-do packs ref. DFES-1505-2005; poster ref. DFES-1691-2005).

▮ REFLECTION

In the first chapters of this book we have considered how to develop ways to ensure continuity and progression in learning languages, through careful planning and liaison. Once the strategies presented above have been considered there is a need to adopt the 'plan, implement, observe, reflect and refine' cycle, so that improvements can be made as part of the process. The next chapter will consider projects which will support continuity and progression, ranging from in-class activities through to large-scale language festivals, jointly organised by primary and secondary.

4. Teachers working together

There are many practical ways in which language teachers in both primary and secondary phases can work to ensure that **continuity and progression** are at the heart of their planning and teaching. Knowing each pupil as an individual, knowing something about his or her background and prior learning, and building on this, a teacher is able to establish a relationship of trust and support and challenge all the pupils in the class. Languages are the same as any other subject area in this respect, but because no single language or approach is used universally, continuity and progression are more complex.

Teachers differentiate in their teaching to involve each individual pupil, using extension and support activities. There are also different ways to support pupils in the Key Stage 2/3 transfer stage, for example through bridging units and top-up classes, either in the primary or secondary school or as a joint venture. There is the possibility of organising collaborative language days for pupils to share their linguistic knowledge and skills. Finally, there is the possibility of staging special events to celebrate language learning and to bring together larger numbers of people involved in teaching and learning languages, along with their colleagues, families and friends. Some of the suggestions below can serve either as a primary-school 'end-of-year' celebration of linguistic achievement, or they can be planned as joint secondary/primary liaison events.

 ## EXTENSION AND SUPPORT ACTIVITIES

In any school or class, there are children who arrive or leave in the middle of the term; some have special educational needs, including gifted-and-talented pupils; some may have different mother tongues or be bilingual in the language being taught; others may have physical disabilities, such as hearing impairment; yet others may not have previously learned a language or may have learned a different language in their last school. In language teaching, where the focus of communication is not English, the need to consider each individual case is particularly important. The following points may be helpful:

- Good communication systems are needed within the school.
  For example, teachers should be able to access background information on children, quickly and easily; Heads of Year should provide early warning of special needs to departments.
- Knowing the individual pupil's background – linguistic, educational and social – will enable the teacher to help the pupil integrate quickly.
  This knowledge is vital to help with planning lessons that take differences into account. Teachers will gain much information from reading the children's Language Portfolios, which they have brought from their primary schools; the new language learners can be provided with Portfolios too, to help them progress up the Languages Ladder.
- A sympathetic teacher will help to reduce anxiety and provide a stress-free environment for language learning.
  This will include providing activities – such as the chorusing of responses – that make the whole group feel included and comfortable.

- Providing a 'buddy' to 'look after', sit next to and befriend newcomers is helpful and pupils usually enjoy the sense of responsibility. Using the buddy and working as a pair can both reinforce learning for the buddy and give confidence to the newcomer (see Chapter 6 for further discussion).

- Remember to allow the 'silent period', described by Krashen (1981), so that pupils can absorb the sounds of the language around them without being forced to speak until they feel ready.

  Language teachers should avoid putting children 'on the spot' by expecting them to perform individual language tasks such as answering a question, when they are not yet ready to do so; they should instead encourage volunteers. The first aim is to build confidence and if motivating activities are provided, volunteers will soon appear. Ideal activities are those that initially require a physical response to show understanding, e.g. miming an action, pointing to a stated item, ticking the correct piece of text.

- Pupils with prior foreign-language skills should be encouraged to take the lead in activities. They could be given the opportunity sometimes to share expressions with the rest of the class, teaching them a phrase, or during the foreign-language lesson telling them what a particular word is in their 'other' language (see also Young Pathfinder 10: *A world of languages*; Datta and Pomphrey 2004). This can build their self-esteem and the respect of fellow pupils, and shows that the skill of learning a foreign language is transferable. Care should be taken, however, not to put pressure on reluctant children who may not wish to be seen as 'different'.

  The level of language knowledge within a class can range from zero to Level 4. Kirsty Pierce, at Marple Hall School, finds that activities engaging the innate ability of children to work things out, galvanise all the children into active participation. This not only builds confidence and knowledge in those with a low level of language, but is also good for pupils with a greater knowledge of the language as they are not, then, the only ones who seem to be speaking in the lessons, Trying to find the missing numbers in a sequence or a quiz, is a good example of this approach; reference sources should be provided.

- Take time to explain to newcomers what has been learnt.

  This could take place in a lunchtime 'catch-up' club or during a differentiated activity, when extension work would be provided for the other pupils.

- Give a summary of the work to be covered to parents of new pupils.

  The information provided could be included by all pupils in their European Language Portfolio. *It could include the vocabulary to be learnt and would make a useful reference sheet for all learners.*

USE OF ICT

The Internet can be both a source of information and a means of exchanging information. Pupils can be paired with 'real' pupils in the other sector, to create a feeling of authenticity in joint projects. In one school, the teacher set up a hotmail address so she could receive and send messages from pupils, who thought their 'penfriend' lived in France! This was her solution to concerns about issues of security/Internet access and anonymity. Her main problem was that she needed to keep good records, as once she had created an imaginary family/situation/pets for each pupil the details had to remain the same! Foreign Language Assistants, sixth formers or supportive native speakers could provide a similar service to local primary pupils.

Teachers can give information to parents about further support available on the Internet, through ICT or in publications. These can be used for reinforcement or extension activities and include:

- the BBC programmes (**www.bbc.co.uk/schools/primaryfrench** and **www.bbc.co.uk/schools/primaryspanish**);
- the CILT publication *Bringing it home* (Farren and Smith 2003), which offers advice to parents about how to support children as they learn languages in primary school, giving lots of ideas of games, songs and activities. For teachers of pupils with a different mother tongue to the majority of their classmates, as well as those who have previously learnt a different foreign language, Young Pathfinder 10: *A world of languages* (Datta and Pomphrey 2004) gives ideas to encourage pupils to appreciate the linguistic and cultural diversity around them.

SECONDARY TOP-UP CLASSES AND TASTER DAYS

Some secondary schools, such as Archbishop Holgate School in York, provide a series of Saturday French sessions for their feeder primary pupils in the summer term of Year 6, to give them basic confidence. These aim to have a different atmosphere to normal school days, but introduce some of the phrases and vocabulary that they will encounter in the following September through games and 'fun' activities.

In many schools, a day is dedicated to bringing together pupils from the clusters of primary schools feeding in to one secondary school. A languages 'taster' activity has traditionally been included in the programme.

Once the children arrive at the secondary school in Year 7, those who have not learned a foreign language may be offered top-up classes, for example in the lunch break. Early setting or fast-tracking may be a solution for the children who have already achieved a high level in a foreign language, e.g. National Curriculum Level 4 in the four skills (see Chapter 6 for further examples).

Foreign Language Assistants may also be part of the link between primary and secondary schools: the cost might be shared between a group of schools, or the Assistant from a secondary school may be used to visit the cluster of primary schools.

An example of working across the phases is provided by Holyhead School, Birmingham. In a six-week project Year 10 students become French 'teachers' in local primary schools for one hour a week. Working with different age groups has been found to have a positive impact on all pupils involved and this project won a European Award for Languages in 2004.

FAMILY LEARNING

In some local education authorities, e.g. City of York Council, East Riding and Nottinghamshire, family learning has been introduced, including a foreign language, often taught on primary school sites. Parents and carers or other adults learn alongside the children, usually after school, and in this way parents become aware of the methodology and the content of the languages classes, and can build on this at home.

 ## BRIDGING UNITS

It was noticeable that where primary and secondary colleagues engaged in joint planning of these units there was both continuity and a greater variety of activities so that pupils' motivation was sustained after transfer.

(*Curriculum continuity,* DfES 2004)

Primary teachers will already be familiar with the concept of bridging units, where pupils in clusters of schools start an activity in Year 6 and complete or present it collaboratively in Year 7 at secondary school.

The chosen timing for the bridging units is usually after the National Key Stage Tests/SATs tests, in the final half-term, when the timetable is less restricted. Many LEAs already expect primary teachers to complete bridging units in core subjects at this time, so the children are familiar with the type of activities involved. For languages, curriculum time can be saved by making the unit cross-curricular and by giving the work a linguistic, cultural or creative focus, for example having an international or European theme, or basing it on the country of their foreign partner school. Joint planning of bridging units benefits not only the pupils but also the teachers, who come together to plan and evaluate the pupils' experiences.

An example of a bridging unit in South Gloucestershire is given on the following page.

CASE STUDY

In South Gloucestershire, languages are taught from Key Stage 1 by non-specialist primary teachers. The report of the International Learning and Research Centre in South Gloucestershire, 'Planning for continuity and progression – a bridging unit for Years 6–7' *(NACELL best practice guide)*, describes the unit of work which builds on links between languages and English in Year 7, through collaboration on aspects of early language learning and literacy with partner primary schools. This bridging unit is based on the QCA non-statutory guidelines for Key Stage 2 in the *National Curriculum handbook for primary teachers in England* (DfES 2000c) and the QCA schemes of work, Units 11 and 12. It establishes whole-school aims as well as a methodological approach and organisational structures for the unit. The aim of the cross-phase unit is 'to draw together teacher expertise and build on pupils' prior learning and transferable language skills, rather than specific foreign-language vocabulary'. Pupils work on the same topic in both English and French for a short time and are assessed by both primary and secondary teachers. They start by marking features on a map and then write directions to different places, drafting and re-drafting and using shared writing techniques to complete their work. The work is trialled in Year 7 and in this way some of the issues of progression and continuity are addressed. Teachers have noted the positive motivation among pupils, who were keen to extend their vocabulary and to demonstrate their skills.

Activity outline:
Areas of language (MFL): Directions and geographical surroundings
Teaching objectives: Write to inform, explain and describe
(from Y7 English framework): Organise texts in appropriate ways

Year 7 programme:
Length of activity: Preparatory week (2–3 hours) plus 3 lessons
Classes:
 Year 7 groups studying French as MFL1 (they are in tutor groups for both MFL and English)
 Each Year 7 group will be linked to a Year 6 class in a partner school
(MFL is French as this is appropriate to partner schools in this case)

Initial resources:
 A video of a route to a recognisable local landmark
 Photographs of key points on the route
 Guidance notes and activity instructions

Week 1: Preparatory lessons
 Identifying conventions and instructional writing (English)
 Directions and associated vocabulary (French)

Week 2:
English
 Lesson 1: watch the video, take notes, prepare a commentary in small groups, compare commentaries to the video
 Lesson 2: write the instructions
French
 Lesson 1: use the notes taken in English lesson 1 to select appropriate and concise equivalents in French, supported by shared writing and a writing frame to scaffold the first attempts
 Lesson 2: write the instructions in French
The instructions are then communicated to the Year 6 classes by post/e-mail/website.
Year 6
 Trial the instructions (e.g. with the video/by a small group following the route/using the photographs) Create a book with commentary in English (descriptive writing) and in French (short sentences as captions).
 Share the book orally and as a shared reading exercise in class (and/or record the commentary).

Other examples of linking activities that may take place during the summer term:

A creative history bridging unit linked Year 6 to Year 7 in a York school, in a project based on World War 2 'evacuees' at the primary school wrote regularly to an identified secondary pupil who played the role of the parent left behind in London in the Blitz. Information for both groups was provided from authentic documents and certain ideas had to be included in each exchange of letters. This idea could be adapted for languages, so that individual pupils in each school are paired and exchange e-mails or letters on a specific theme, e.g. a journey or an imaginary holiday. Pupils might talk in simple French (*j'aime/je n'aime pas*, etc) about food at a VE Day street party, but use English to discuss the event in more detail. Penpals in Years 5/6 might link with Years 8/9, with the older pupils being imaginary French children with families, who write in simple French about the differences and similarities of living in a town, etc. Such work might be combined with work on a place like La Réunion, or draw on the pupils' imagination by creating imaginary monster families. Similarly postcards or e-mails could be sent as if one group were travelling around the world and the other group were at home asking questions at a simple level, e.g. about the weather, the food, etc.

A cluster of schools in the East Riding of Yorkshire has developed a bridging unit based on language awareness and European awareness. The materials can be found at **www.eriding.net/mfl/bridging_unit.shtml**.

Un pays francophone – QCA *Scheme of work*, Unit 12

This final unit of the QCA *Scheme of work* (QCA 2000a) can be used at the end of Year 6 and the beginning of Year 7 either as a bridging unit or to be completed in primary school. It allows primary pupils to celebrate, consolidate and demonstrate what they have learnt. Secondary colleagues or former pupils now in Year 7 may be invited to see a presentation or judge displays. Unit 12 draws on all the topics and vocabulary covered in the preceding units of the QCA *Scheme of work*, but aims to encourage independent work so that children can extend their linguistic horizons and work creatively. The unit is based on a theme which takes them out of the classroom context into a new environment, where they can use real language to research and present what they have discovered about a francophone location. Pupils from different feeder schools are all able to contribute, even those who have not previously learned the language, as they can work in English to complete their investigation.

Unit 12 provides many opportunities for cross-curricular study, with potential links to:

*   Geography (e.g. discussing maps, climate, handling class sets of volcanic lava);
*   History (e.g. datelines, traditional stories, pirates);
*   Music (e.g. singing traditional songs, playing different musical instruments);
*   Citizenship (comparison of family life and responsibilities);
*   R.E. (e.g. comparing places of worship, religious festivals);
*   Food Technology (e.g. tasting exotic fruits, making a traditional dish);

- Art and Design (themed collage, making models of homes);
- ICT (e.g. desktop publishing of publicity brochure);
- Dance and Drama (e.g. re-enactment of traditional folk tale, sega dance).

Unit 12 can also include the cultural dimension of imaginary travel to a foreign country and allow pupils, teachers and parents to share new knowledge about the country and its people. These intercultural aspects of language learning form a central part of the strategy in the *Key Stage 2 Framework*. La Réunion is suggested as a possible focus for pupils learning French and Morocco is also interesting because of its Muslim culture, which can add an extra inter-faith dimension to the work. Teachers could use their own contacts and travels on which to base the work, as these add a real element of authenticity. The British Council (**www.britishcouncil.org**) and the Centre for Global Education (**www.yorksj.ac.uk**) are also potential sources of links, ideas and themes. Local universities and teacher-training institutions may also have foreign staff and students willing to be interviewed or give a short presentation in the target language. In this unit, pupils can work at their own linguistic level using all four language skills, but all contribute to a shared event such as a Primary Languages Day (see Chapter 5).

Resources might include:

maps, a globe, bilingual dictionaries, tourist brochures, postcards, artefacts from the country, scanned photos, samples of local recipes and foods, audio tapes or CDs of traditional music.

Pupils might:

- do research on the Internet and contribute to a presentation;
- work independently, in groups, or as a class to create models, brochures, poster displays and dramatic, dance or musical presentations;
- recreate a simulated flight to the chosen country;
- make a traditional dish using a simplified recipe in the target language.

© The late Harold Robinson

SPECIAL EVENTS

The events in this chapter can involve individual schools, clusters of primaries or primary and secondary school partnerships.

After National Key Stage Tests (SATs) and the May half-term, there is more flexibility in the timetable to organise and plan joint events with other schools. This period is also when both primary and secondary schools include whole-class, whole-year or whole-school activities in the timetable.

One example of an activity which could be used at this time of year to emphasise the diversity of languages all around us would be to follow the ideas of the 'World of Languages' competition. This was run by CILT and sponsored by the Nuffield Foundation in 2003 and was devised by a group of teacher trainers from across Europe, who were working on the Socrates 'Primary Letter Box' project. This project investigated the teaching of reading in the foreign language in the primary school and the competition challenged pupils to make a display in material they found around them, which illustrated the diversity of languages which surround us. An archive of competition entries can be viewed at **www.nacell.org.uk/home/worldoflanguages.htm**. Teachers might like to use this idea in their school or in a cluster of schools to raise awareness about language learning.

Many schools include a **European Day** in the year, where the emphasis is often on language awareness and can involve the whole school. Each class might choose a different European country and demonstrate an aspect of the language or culture, e.g. greetings, food, a region or geography, traditional costumes or dance performance. The **European Day of Languages**, 26 September, is often chosen as the date for a special languages event. As it falls at the start of the English school year, this is an ideal time to celebrate languages and publicise what is happening in schools.

Individual schools might celebrate a festival such as Bastille Day, *le 14 juillet*, *Fasching* or *fiestas*, using Year 7 pupils from the secondary school to help run a carousel of activities. These could include the following:

Preparation

- *Les invitations*: Decide who you are going to invite, if anybody e.g. the Headteacher, caretaker, Foreign Language Assistant. Write the list. Group activity: Write and decorate an invitation to a chosen guest. The invitation can then be placed in an envelope and addressed.
- *Le menu*: List the food the children will be having. Group activity: Write and illustrate a menu.
- *Le programme*: List all the activities that will be available to celebrate the day, explaining them as you do so. Group activity: Design and illustrate a programme.

On the day

- A *boules* tournament with a (simple) score sheet in French
- Karaoke to favourite foreign-language songs
- Learn a traditional French song
- Tasting of typical food associated with a country of the foreign language
- Cooking, e.g. making *crêpes*
- 'Buying' food at a café, with photocopies of menus
- Creating and writing differentiated postcards to send home
- Play Bingo
- Learn a French country dance
- Guess the country: The children can refer to a copy of a map of Europe. Say the vowels in a country for the children to guess the country. Compare the English and French versions of the names of the countries.
- Elimination game: Write down the names of towns from a map of France on a set of cards. Take one card at a time from the pile and hold it concealed from the class. Ask one group at a time to stand. Give each individual a choice of two places and ask them to guess the right one. '*C'est Paris ou Bordeaux?*' / '*Paris?*' / '*Non! Eliminé!*' Those who are eliminated sit down, those remaining stand at the front. Keep doing this until only one pupil is left. A volunteer picks a card for the group to 'visit'.
- Rhyming countries: Children can use an encyclopaedia, map, dictionary or computer to find foreign-language names for countries and try to find ones that rhyme. They could make up a song using the rhyming places, set to a familiar tune.
- *Eurostations*: Spread out hoops, named after countries on the hall floor. The children jump in and out of the 'countries' until they are told to stop. If the name of the country they are in is then called, they are out.
- *Concours de l'Europe*: Let the children organise a Eurovision Song Contest or sports tournament, in which they represent their country of choice.
- *Naufrage* (Shipwreck): Set the context for the game as you wish. Teach the class the various commands you will give. Decide which of the four walls of the hall is the closest to North and point to the four walls, naming them *le nord, le sud, l'est, l'ouest*. Limit yourself to a few instructions, chosen from the list below:

Le nord, le sud, l'est, l'ouest	jump to face the correct direction
A gauche/A droite	port/starboard – go to that side
A l'avant/A l'arrière	bow/stern – go to the front or back of the hall
Salut Capitaine	(Captain's coming) – salute
Bateaux de sauvetage	(lifeboats) – get into groups of three
Néttoyez bien le pont	scrub the deck
Un homme à la mer	(man/woman overboard) – make a piggy-back
Grimper le gréement	(climb the rigging) – climb
Sous-marin	(submarine) lie down, legs in the air

- Paint mixing represented by coloured blobs and mathematical signs or text, labelled in French, e.g. *bleu et jaune font vert*. An experiment could be conducted to shine torches through coloured transparencies and recorded in a similar way.

At Hornsea School in the East Riding of Yorkshire, in July 2004, all Year 6 primary pupils from the secondary's feeder schools were invited to attend a series of workshops co-ordinated by the secondary school but staffed by experts from the county. Primary teachers attended as supporters and carers, rather than taking an active teaching role themselves.

For several years in York, primary teachers in feeder schools of Joseph Rowntree Secondary School took the lead role in the organisation of a Primary Languages Afternoon, using the secondary school sports hall as a venue. In the carousel of activities primary and secondary colleagues worked alongside each other and other co-opted adults to lead activities. Primary pupils also staged a 'performance' to start or end the afternoon, for example a fashion show, with a pupil describing the outfits. This was particularly successful in involving male models! Year 6 pupils prepared for this activity separately in their own schools, but the focus vocabulary was taught at the event, to all the pupils taking part from the whole cluster.

Trainee teacher leads a tasting activity as part of the carousel

In Tameside the PRISM (Primary in Secondary Modern Languages) team organised a travelling *Miniville* in secondary school halls, involving several clusters of primary schools, which brought their pupils to experience a 'Day in France'. A French 'town' would be set up, with stage flats made by the Technology department of a local secondary school and peopled by Foreign Language Assistants. The children had opportunities to practise language they had learnt during the year and had their passports stamped for each activity, including changing their money and buying food and drink in a French café.

There are many possible types of special events: they might take the form of a music or story-telling workshop, an international Christmas carol concert, or a treasure hunt. Other ideas for a focus might include: making a radio or TV magazine programme, organising a cookery demonstration, interviewing 'famous people' or presenting the weather forecast in the foreign language.

Pupils from Easington School, East Riding of Yorkshire present some language activities at a primary languages conference

As a way to bring together different ages and groups of language learners and native speakers, from young children and family groups through to over-sixties, one Comenius centre organised a mini-languages challenge. In an informal situation, with glasses of juice or wine, contestants were given a choice of challenges at three levels, timed for 30 minutes. In the 'easy' challenge, they simply had to learn to say 'hello' in as many different languages as possible. At the next level, they were asked to learn to say and tick off from a list a variety of phrases in a new language, with confident 'teachers' or native speakers supporting them. The challenge for those with some prior language skill involved amusing tasks to be completed in the target language. Winners were identified, persuaded to 'perform' to the audience and prizes awarded.

LANGUAGE FESTIVALS, PERFORMANCES AND REGIONAL EVENTS

Increasing numbers of LEAs, Comenius centres, Specialist Language Colleges, initial teacher-training institutions and groups of schools have organised workshops and performances on a bigger scale, for example to celebrate the European Day of Languages, on 26 September. The East Riding of Yorkshire holds an international concert on that date, with performances from a joint school choir and by individual schools. This is motivating and enjoyable for both performers and audience. Concert workshops with Detlev Jöcker, the German composer and performer who has written many songs especially for foreign primary pupils learning German, have been a great success on his UK tours. His visits have been preceded by musical and language workshops so that the actual performance can be as interactive and valuable as possible. Apart from the value of allowing large numbers of pupils from different schools to work together his workshops have stimulated an interest in German, which is taught more often in secondary schools than primary. For primary pupils who do not learn German, taking an active part in a song workshop in German has been a particularly positive experience. It has also been a good opportunity to bring in secondary pupils from Year 7, who have just started German, so that they can participate alongside Year 6 pupils from their old schools.

Detlev Jöcker leads an interactive concert in German

Other 'big events' have focused on drama workshops and performances by theatre groups such as the European Theatre Company or Abracadabra, which offer activities for both primary and secondary pupils. If the language content is known in advance, and the pupils well prepared, a combined event could be arranged for both primary and lower secondary pupils. This would reduce the costs for each school involved, as well as bringing both pupils and teachers together in an enjoyable context. Even without support from professional singers or actors, a gifted teacher may be able to create an activity for a wider audience. An AST primary liaison teacher at Easingwold (secondary) School in North Yorkshire wrote a fairy tale to be performed by sixth-form students to an audience of primary pupils. The simple script included lots of repetitive features, so that there could be audience participation. The story told how an old couple, who had been caring for several foster children from different countries, had run out of money and turned the children out into the forest to fend for themselves. The children got lost and came across various animals. Each animal spoke a different language and so a different child each time was able to ask the way in the appropriate language and understand the response. It was therefore the children's collective ability to speak foreign languages which eventually saved them and they lived happily ever after!

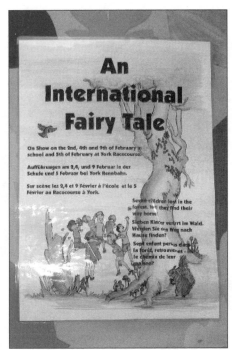

Pupils from Easingwold Secondary School perform for primary pupils as part of a fairy story project

Special events such as the European Year of Languages in 2001 brought together language learners of all ages and backgrounds. Yorktalk2001, a day of language activities sponsored by the Nuffield Foundation, was a catalyst to create networks and links between local primary and secondary schools, as well as other providers of language courses such as the Goethe-Institut, the Alliance Française, local universities, colleges and communities of native speakers. The day included performances of sketches; plays; songs; dances by Nepalese dancers from the local Ghurka regiment; music, including African drumming and rock songs composed especially by local sixth-formers; an exhibition about learning languages and a parade through the streets of York by pupils carrying brightly coloured balloons, which were released together when the parade met the Lord Mayor. The balloon tags had individual messages written in more than 50 different languages by pupils and VIPs, including Professor Eric Hawkins. Local shops and restaurants took part by providing clues for a treasure hunt in their shop windows, or by providing prizes such as a free meal in a Mexican restaurant if the customer tried to speak Spanish throughout. Events such as this depend on teamwork and are challenging to stage, but there are immeasurable benefits in bringing together so many people involved in languages for a common and successful purpose. They are also very motivating for the pupils who take part, who see that they share a common skill and interest with many other people.

'Yorktalk 2001': York pupils with
balloons bearing messages in
different languages

There are many other examples of large-scale language events to draw on. The *NACELL best practice guide* gives details of organising a languages festival by the Liverpool team of primary MFL teachers and the Liverpool Education and Lifelong Learning Service. The article explains that a language festival is a means of promoting community involvement:

> *A typical festival provides pupils with opportunities to speak on their own in front of an audience, to speak in groups or present whole-class activities and to sing songs or perform dance to music. These events can be fruitful in building bridges with the community and in offering the pupils a chance to demonstrate their confidence in language work.*
>
> (*NACELL best practice guide*)

The Liverpool team provides a checklist for organising the event which includes writing invitations to parents and carers, taking care of guests, and in-depth preparation of language activities so that pupils can speak with confidence and enjoy the event.

A list of possible in-house activities is given, such as a spoken language festival and an open day, along with a list of people who can help, advice on how to make the event a success (e.g. keep it the right length, have a good opener) and suggestions for both non-competitive and competitive activities to include.

REFLECTION

The many benefits that can result from such collaborative events include increased motivation and self-confidence of the pupils, improved continuity and progression in the language, better communication and liaison between teachers in different Key Stages and greater awareness and involvement of the wider community.

A detailed example of working as a team to stage a Primary Languages Day follows in Chapter 5.

5. Bringing children together – a Primary Languages Day

We saw in the previous chapter that collaborating in joint primary/secondary events gives an unparalleled opportunity to staff and children to foster relationships, build confidence and work together to provide continuity and progression in the foreign language. This chapter will look in detail at how such an event can be organised.

There are many factors to take into account when organising a languages day, including focus, location, timing, staff and finances. The event we present here was created for local feeder schools, to give them the opportunity to come together in the secondary school and to give them a positive and stimulating language-learning experience. The aim of the day was to build self-confidence and motivation and to introduce simple language in an exciting context, consolidating key phrases and vocabulary.

Examples of materials used, including the timetable for the day, quizzes, worksheets, words of songs, etc can be found in Appendix 2: 'Resources'.

Working in a carousel and mixing up school groups

© The late Geoff Arthur

WHY?

Primary schools often rely on a single teacher to deliver the foreign language, who may work in a relatively isolated situation, even within a cluster of schools. Having a specific reason to contact other local schools and to work with secondary colleagues who are going to receive their Year 6 pupils is valuable, both for the teachers involved and inevitably for their pupils. Primary pupils also work on the foreign language in a rather isolated situation and the added motivation, confidence and self-esteem gained by joining up with other pupils with a common purpose is beneficial to them, too. When these pupils arrive at language classes as Year 7 pupils in the following September, they will already have shared a common activity and be more at ease with each other, in addition to recognising their 'new' teacher.

Sharing common activities shows children that languages are about communication and that learning a language helps them to communicate with others who share that language. In some cases, pupils may not all have had the same language background and a wide range of both ability and experience may be involved in the event. With careful planning to include revision of key phrases or vocabulary, pupils with less experience of learning the language can begin to acquire some knowledge and skills in a stress-free situation, thus increasing their motivation towards further language learning. The Primary Languages Day can also serve as a training event for primary teachers, who will observe different styles and teaching ideas. Teachers may also wish to use it as an assessment or moderation opportunity, supported by secondary colleagues. Parents might be invited and secondary pupils used as support, thus underlining the networks involved in lifelong learning.

WHERE?

These events may be held in a secondary school, even if the day's activities are run by primary teachers, as there is often more space and it also gives pupils a 'real' experience of the site, finding their way there, moving around, meeting pupils and staff. Older pupils can be used as helpers and an added bonus could be the secondary Head or representative giving a welcome speech – in the target language, if possible!

Children at an interactive language day performance

WHO?

STAFF

The co-ordinator will need to find staff for the event. Apart from primary and secondary colleagues, other staff with foreign-language competence will be required. This is a good opportunity to involve Foreign Language Assistants, teaching assistants, native speakers (e.g. parents, friends), sixth formers and students from local colleges and universities. For students on both primary and secondary teacher-training programmes, assisting at a Primary Languages Day is a wonderful way to experience primary languages first hand. All of these people can be actively involved. It may also be possible to bring in experts from outside the local area (for example CILT Associate trainers who can be found via **www.nacell.org.uk/profdev/cat.htm**). It is important to build on the strengths of each member of the team, for example there may be someone with a talent in music or drama whose skills might be utilised. In addition to speakers of the foreign language, other helpers will be required and may include other teaching staff, parents and older pupils. Year 7 pupils gain a sense of responsibility when they are asked to look after a group of Year 6 pupils for the day, with the added benefit to primary pupils who recognise friendly faces in the following September.

Involving other adults who speak the target language to organise an activity reduces the load

CHILDREN

The numbers of pupils and teachers/supporters involved will depend on the size of the venue, the numbers of pupils transferring and the stamina of the organiser! The secondary hall or sports hall is often available from May to July, when exams are over and some of the classrooms may be free after the departure of the sixth form or GCSE groups. At Malton and Norton, for example, in North Yorkshire, around 500 pupils attend a Primary Languages Day each year, hosted alternately by one of the secondary schools and co-ordinated by a team of primary and secondary teachers, but also involving a large number of other adults, such as parents, native speakers and teacher-training students.

WHEN?

The most common time to stage a primary languages event is during the final half-term, in May, June or July, after SATs and when the timetable is traditionally more flexible (as explained in

Chapter 4). There is also great benefit to be had, however, in choosing an earlier part of the year, provided accommodation is available. Rather than a celebration of the 'end' of the primary phase and the 'start' of the secondary experience, a collaborative event can be integrated into the primary programme, bringing cluster schools together for a particular purpose or as part of a regular collaboration. This allows the primary teacher to reap the benefit of the increased focus and motivation that such an event brings. Whenever the event is held, it is important to have a rationale and to prepare the pupils in advance. Planning well ahead will ensure that there are no clashes of dates with the many events which take place in the summer term, such as sports days, school trips and secondary liaison days. It will also ensure that the adults involved are available and are certain of their roles.

The co-ordinator will need to decide whether to hold a whole or half-day event, liaising with colleagues. The decision may be influenced by schools' diaries, transport arrangements and costs, arrangements for lunch or refreshments, availability of staff, the language focus and content of the session or even the weather! For example, if a *boules* contest is to be included in the programme, it is clearly less likely to be cancelled in the summer.

Pupils in Ripon wait for the French afternoon to start

How?

CHECKLIST

The first step to organising a Primary Languages Day is to decide on a co-ordinator. Once the co-ordinator has been identified and contact details exchanged with key players, an early meeting can delegate responsibilities. The checklist below provides a useful *aide-mémoire* for staging such an event.

	Action	Completed/ Not required
1	Administrative/secretarial support identified	
2	Date chosen, with an alternative	
3	Venue chosen, e.g. whether a primary school, secondary school, or college	

4	Number of pupils involved and the ratio of staff to pupils, plus adult supporters decided upon. (A manageable group size for workshops and games is 10–20 pupils if each pupil is to be actively involved and to derive the maximum benefit from the opportunity. There should be an allocation of 2 adults to each group of 20 pupils and one named teacher responsible for each school group)	
5	Age range of pupils involved decided upon. (It is difficult to organise a big event of this type if pupils are from different year groups, but in small rural schools, for example, with mixed-year classes it may be necessary to build in appropriate differentiation to include younger pupils)	
6	Aims and a theme for the event chosen, if appropriate	
7	Dates fixed for team meetings	
8	Transport arrangements made	
9	Safety risk assessments made, including fire and emergency procedures	
10	Letters sent to parents, including cost, health and dietary notes	
11	Programme drafted (and eventually produced and distributed to the team) with roles and responsibilities for each team member and suggested timing of each activity if a carousel or workshops are to be used; length of lunchtime or breaks determined	
12	Sponsorship requested, if appropriate (see below)	
13	Lunch and refreshment arrangements made, including lunch-time supervision. (If a packed meal is planned, a different dining area may be required. Sponsorship may fund 'themed' food such as *baguettes* and Orangina, but pupils' individual health requirements may mean that it is easier for pupils to provide their own packed lunch if the event is for a whole day)	
14	Toilet arrangements sorted out, including disabled access	
15	Signs provided to rooms and areas being used	
16	Furniture needs and seating arrangements determined; technical support, e.g. loud speakers, microphones, video-recording or digital photography of the event; what will be used to indicate a change of activity, e.g. bell, etc	
17	Pupil passports produced and staffing of 'passport control' planned (see below and example in Appendix 2)	
18	Resources required listed	
19	'Teachers' and 'helpers' listed, e.g. KS3 or Y10 helpers can be used as group leaders or 'buddies' who will look out for 'their' group when they start secondary school	
20	List compiled of attendees by school	
21	Certificate of attendance produced for each pupil involved (to be presented later, e.g. at a school assembly (see Appendix 2))	
22	Invitations sent to Headteachers and other VIPs and possibly the press (these should include a clear brief with timings)	
23	All those who may need to know notified, including ground staff, administrative staff, school traffic patrols, etc. (It is important to take safety into account with extra coaches or pedestrians arriving at and departing from the venue)	
24	Introduction and conclusion of the event planned (remember to thank the key supporters, e.g. with a small gift for the back-stage workers; write letters of thanks afterwards)	

FUNDING AND SPONSORSHIP

Some funding for these events may be available in Pathfinder LEAs, or when a Specialist Language College is involved. Other funding may be accessible from the Nuffield Foundation, Excellence in Cities Action Zones, or local sponsors. A chocolate manufacturer in York sponsors the Malton/Norton days mentioned above, with money for lunch as well as a bag of chocolates for each participant. If sufficient funding is available, it might be possible to budget for a small pocket dictionary for each pupil. If these are purchased in advance, the inclusion of a dictionary quiz or activity (see Appendix 2) is a valuable addition to the programme. It also acts as a calming activity in an otherwise physically active day. Publishers may be persuaded to provide materials to support the teaching or to offer small prizes for these events, which will increase pupils' motivation on the day.

OTHER PRACTICAL CONSIDERATIONS

- It is important to create a **master file** with all the essential information about the event, the programme, with times and room numbers, names of staff and support staff assisting them, the pupils' details, including health notes, e.g. allergies, contact numbers, names and gender of pupils from each school, etc. This folder should be accessible in a central location. A reduced version of the key details should be given to each member of staff.
- **Catering** should be organised well in advance, not forgetting to provide refreshments and cups for observers, pupils and staff involved, rubbish bags and paper towels.
- **Toilets** for use by the visiting adults and pupils should be clearly signposted, and comfort breaks scheduled in the programme.
- **Signs** should be prepared for (and, if necessary, to show the way to) all the rooms, with timings, staff and activities listed. Toilets, dining rooms, exits and fire exits will also need labels, as will the 'passport-control' point where pupils will register on arrival.
- **Complete sets of teaching resources** will need to be prepared and labelled for each teacher or activity leader, including for example, flashcards, game boards, dice, counters, tapes, worksheets, spare pencils, scissors, board markers, tape, Post-its, glue-sticks, blutack, etc.
- **Choice of common vocabulary**: One important thing to do once the team has been established, is to agree a focus of language to be used. This will include both the everyday/organisational language, as well as the vocabulary needed to play the games, to change group, to go through 'customs' (see below) or for the focus of the day. At events in Ripon, York and Aylesbury, primary teachers were asked to ensure that all pupils had been introduced to a minimum list of phrases and words, so that they were immediately able to recognise and use these. The vocabulary might be as simple as numbers 1–20, colours and greetings, but by identifying a common language base, all activities could build on the same prior knowledge.
- **Passport-control resources** will include pupil/school lists, sticky labels or colour-coded name badges to hand to each pupil once their passport has been checked and a few individual questions or greetings exchanged. Pupils can make their own passports in their primary schools, before coming to the day. This is the point at which it is easy to re-mix school groups for the carousel of activities, by giving only a few pupils in the passport queue the same colour badge or by using different colour stickers for every four pupils. This ensures that the pupils will know someone in their group, while introducing them to new faces.

Passport control

- **Money/*Bureau de change***: Some Primary Language Days have included a *Bureau de change*, where pupils exchange a small amount of money or tokens for plastic Euros and *centimes*. (These can be purchased quite cheaply in large French toy shops or hypermarkets and through some educational suppliers.) Having some foreign currency allows the programme to include practice of the appropriate conversations to purchase small items of food and drink – or indeed lunch – postcards, stickers, pens or foreign sweets, souvenirs, comics, etc. Again, these could be bulk-purchased abroad in advance.
- **Technical support**: Older pupils or sixth formers may be enlisted to assist with sound, videos, photography, etc. They may also be responsible for the timing of activity changes, by playing a familiar tune or bell through the loud speakers to signal the change-over. The first few bars of the *Marseillaise* provide a useful signal for French-themed events.
- **Staff/supporter identification**: It is helpful when there are so many new faces to identify staff and supporters clearly. Colourful customised t-shirts could be worn, or simply large name labels in co-ordinated colours, e.g. French flag background with '*Je peux t'aider*' or Italian flag with '*Posso aiutarla*'.
- **Publicity**: Too often we forget to publicise what we do, but the local media may be more easily persuaded to attend big events such as Primary Languages Days than smaller events at individual schools. It is easy enough to record the day with a series of digital photos or digital video. These can be downloaded and put onto the school or LEA website. The videos would also be a useful source of material for future training sessions. Once again, the help of older pupils, even non-linguists, could be elicited to take the role of reporter for such an event.

WHAT?

Deciding on a theme or topic for a Primary Languages Day can be both exciting and challenging. In this section we will illustrate in detail the format of a day which has been successfully run several times. These practical ideas could be adapted to local needs. The examples are in French, but can be easily translated into other languages.

The theme of a visit to the zoo was chosen, as this had a primary focus and most of the words are similar in French and English. It was written to include greetings, picnic and animal vocabulary, animal sounds and plenty of interactivity with pupils.

A VISIT TO THE ZOO

At Aylesbury Specialist Language College, in 2002 and 2003, a group of representatives from each feeder primary school was invited to attend the Primary Languages Day and volunteer sixth-form students assumed a support role. Secondary teachers undertook the organisation and liaison roles, primary teachers ensured their pupils' welfare and behaviour, and experts were brought in to lead the workshop activities. This division of labour meant that the event was transportable and could have been repeated in different venues if numbers of pupils or transport difficulties at one site had been a problem.

Pupils follow the story

Timetable for the day

Overleaf there is a sample timetable for a Primary Languages Day which involved 60 pupils. With carousels of activities and more teachers, larger groups could be accommodated. Appendix 2 includes full details of the activities which follow.

PROGRAMME POUR LE 03 JUILLET

Groupe Blanc : D7 avec Rosemary Bevis
Mrs McVean, Mrs Shorrocks and Miss Howson

10.00	Arrive; go to Harding Hall with Passport ready
10.15	Introductions / programme for the day
10.30 – 11.00	Flashcard games
11.00 – 11.15	Break (picnic area if fine)
11.45 – 12.15	Make Snake
12.15 – 1.05	Lunch in Dining Room Boules (on grass by picnic area if fine, in gym if wet)
1.05 – 1.35	Dictionary quiz
1.35 – 2.05	Board Game
2.05 – 2.15	Short Break (pupils to loo or stay in D7)
2.15 – 2.50	Visite au zoo
2.50 – 3.00	Certificates / prizes; clear up & depart

On arrival, the children pass through passport control and are given coloured name badges. Initially, they assemble together, possibly in a large hall, where they can be welcomed and be given safety instructions, advice about toilets, litter and ground rules for break and lunchtimes, when they should be supervised by their own teachers. The children are then divided into groups according to their coloured badges.

There is a short break after the Introductory session. Then the groups go into the workshop sessions where they complete two of the four reinforcement activities, each lasting about 30 minutes, in order to maintain their concentration. The other two activities are then completed after the lunch break. During the lunch break a *boules* competition is held, outside if the weather is fine, or in the gym if wet, modifying the traditional game with soft balls and target hoops, which attract a different number of points when the ball lands inside the hoop. This introduction to French culture has proved very popular with pupils, as well as allowing them to expend surplus energy before the afternoon workshops.

All the activities are planned to reinforce the key phrases and vocabulary through songs and games, culminating in the *grande finale*. One of the aims of the day is for teachers to keep in the target language as much as possible, to demonstrate activities and use gestures and lots of repetition. It is important to gain the confidence of the children first before encouraging them to 'have a go', and not to pressurise them into responding until they are comfortable with the activities and the sounds, especially if they are being taught by a stranger in an unfamiliar environment.

Introductory vocabulary session

You will need:

- flashcards of zoo animals;
- flashcards of picnic items.

The first session, using traditional flashcard games (see Appendix 2), introduces and reinforces key vocabulary to ensure that all pupils are able to take an active part in the day. For more ideas on games see Young Pathfinder 2: *Games and fun activities* (Martin 1995).

Workshops

1. *Song session*

You will need:

- OHTs of the songs;
- overhead projector.

During the song session (see Appendix 2 for song lyrics), all the key vocabulary that pupils will be learning, or have learnt in the earlier flashcard games session, is recycled in familiar tunes or in nonsense songs, e.g. the names of some zoo animals to the tune of 'Here we go round the mulberry bush', or a variation of 'If you're happy and you know it, clap your hands', using picnic food and drink. Pupils who are not yet confident enough to repeat the sounds of new words can listen to the others and join in with the actions. For further help in creating songs, see CILT Young Pathfinder 6: *Let's join in!* (Cheater and Martin 1998).

2. *Dictionary quiz*

> You will need:
>
> * dictionaries;
> * dictionary quiz sheets (tailored to the dictionary you are using);
> * pencils.

The dictionary quiz session (see Appendix 2) encourages children to find their way around a bilingual dictionary. It is essential for them to have exactly the same dictionary and edition for this activity, as page numbers will be crucial. Even pupils who have not used a bilingual dictionary before will begin to find their way around a simple pocket version within thirty minutes, with a little support. The answers to all the clues are names of zoo animals or items from the picnic, which they have met before orally and will meet again at the end of the day. Being able to use a bilingual dictionary is an invaluable skill (cf *National Literacy Strategy* and *Key Stage 2 Framework for Languages*). In addition to the dictionary quiz (which has definitive answers and so can be used to attract prizes for the highest correct scores), pupils can be given a word search which will also focus on the key vocabulary of the day.

3. *Puppet workshop*

> You will need:
>
> * photocopies of the snake head (see right);
> * one clean sock per pupil;
> * double-sided tape;
> * scissors;
> * colouring pens or pencils.

In this practical session, children make a simple snake glove puppet out of a sock (see Appendix 2 for instructions). The materials should be prepared in advance, so that the teacher can maximise the use of the target language, thereby avoiding wasting time cutting out paper and the subsequent mess. The instructions should be given in the target language, so pupils will have the opportunity to hear the foreign language for an authentic purpose. As the activity involves making a puppet, the pupils have a visual model to follow and kinaesthetic learners are catered for. Once a pair of pupils have completed their puppets, they should be encouraged to engage in a simple conversation with their neighbours, using the puppets to create a dialogue in the foreign language.

Using known greetings and personal questions such as *Bonjour/Ça va?/Comment t'appelles-tu?/Quel âge as-tu?/Au revoir*, etc and the appropriate responses, the teacher can model a dialogue using puppets and encourage pupils to work in pairs so the puppets speak to each other. In this way, pupils are less anxious about using the language, as it is the puppets and not themselves who are talking. They can try out different tones, e.g. voice and expression, bringing the dialogue alive. This will add to the pupils' confidence orally, as well as establishing contact with new friends.

4. *Board game*

You will need:

- copies of the board game (see below; one per group of two to four children);
- game tick sheet (see overleaf);
- pencils;
- dice;
- counters.

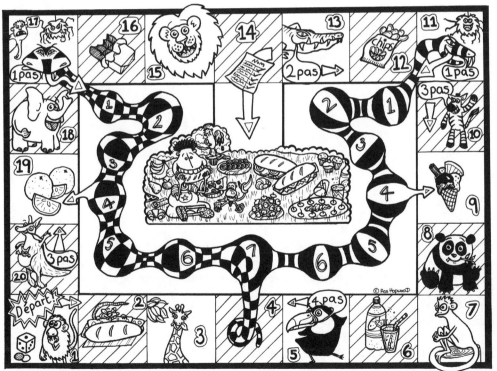

The board game (see Appendix 2) is based loosely on 'Snakes and ladders'. Pupils can be taught the basic vocabulary and phrases for playing a board game, e.g. 'it's your turn', 'six steps', 'I've won', etc. They will already be familiar with the rules of 'Snakes and ladders' and should soon pick up the way to play. Each player has a picnic 'shopping list' (see right) and the aim is to throw dice and move counters around the board, going up and down snakes, but also collecting ticks each time they land on an item on their list (e.g. *une limonade*, *un sandwich*, *un paquet de chips*, etc). The winner is the first pupil to complete a full picnic list. In a 30-minute slot, it is possible to play the game more than once and this is provided for on the tick sheet. Children enjoy playing and learning at the same time and so they should be relaxed and confident enough to read out the name of the article from their list as they land on it.

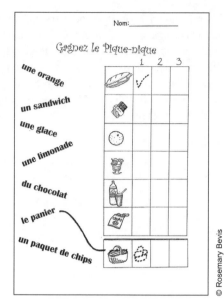

© Rosemary Bevis

5. *Grande finale*

You will need:

- overhead projector;
- large screen;
- OHTs of each zoo animal;
- flashcards of animals
- soft toy of each zoo animal;
- picnic basket;

- 'zoo': box or crate;
- picnic items;
- large puppet, i.e. Bernard;
- cassette player;
- cassette of animal noises.

The children will need:

- snake sock puppets – one per child.

The final event of the day is the staging of an interactive production of the 'Visit to the zoo'. This will usually be in a large hall, with the pupils seated facing a screen. All the pupils by this time have a glove-puppet snake and should be able to join in confidently, using the key vocabulary.

The presenter introduces a large cuddly toy dog, Bernard (or other puppet of your choice), who is carrying a picnic basket and going to the zoo for his birthday treat, but is terrified of snakes. It is important to realise at this point that the target language has been used for the whole day as much as possible and despite this the pupils should still be alert, concentrating and enjoying themselves. The children are encouraged to sing 'Happy birthday' to Bernard in French and are then taught several actions that they have to perform every time they hear key words:

- *'serpent'* – point their glove-puppet snakes at Bernard and hiss;
- *'pique-nique'* – rub their tummies and say *'miam, miam'*;
- *'visiter le zoo'* – 'walk their fingers' through the air;
- *'Ecoutez!'* – cup their hand to their ear;
- *'Qu'est-ce que c'est?'* – hold up their hands, gasp and say *'Oh là là!'*.

The articles in the picnic basket are identified, repeating the vocabulary from earlier sessions in the day. Using a repetition-style marching song (see Appendix 2), in which pupils repeat back a line to the presenter, the food vocabulary can be quickly revised and the picnic replaced in the basket for later use.

The presenter then 'takes' Bernard to the zoo: part of a picture of a zoo animal is shown on the overhead projector and the noise of the animal is played on tape, as Bernard approaches each 'cage'. (A PowerPoint presentation could also be used for this activity.) The presenter asks *'Qu'est-ce que c'est?'* and as the picture is gradually revealed, children should be encouraged to identify the animal, after first teasing Bernard by hissing and pointing their snakes at him, as every time he hears a noise he thinks it is a snake (*hiss!*). After the animal has been correctly identified, the reward is for that member of the audience to be called to the front, be given a small cuddly toy of the animal and asked to stand in line alongside the other animals as they appear. After each new animal is identified Bernard is keen to get to his picnic (*'miam, miam'*), but he is always told he has to continue with his visit to the zoo first (walk fingers). As all the animals eventually appear, they are 'transformed' into a line of children holding the appropriate cuddly toys and the *dénouement* takes place: the monkeys have stolen the picnic and are eating it up – poor Bernard! But he is then given an ice cream in consolation! As the 'animals' return to their cages, the pupils can be encouraged to say goodbye (*'Au revoir girafe!'*, *'Au revoir lion!'*, etc).

The snake puppets hiss at Bernard

Bernard is the star of the show

© Rosemary Bevis

▮ REFLECTION

The pupil feedback from these days has always been positive. Not only have they worked together in mixed-school groups, but they have also met different teachers and begun to realise that learning a language opens doors to new ways of communicating. With a very limited number of phrases and vocabulary and careful planning, pupils have gained or reinforced new skills – not only listening and speaking skills, but also limited reading and writing. They have participated in a 'fun' activity, which will hopefully motivate them to develop further their linguistic competence.

For the primary and secondary teachers, this type of event provides an opportunity to observe different teaching styles and activities which can be copied, to work together with a shared goal, alongside pupils they have taught or will teach and even to assess their achievement informally.

The final chapter will give teachers ideas for appropriate methodology which supports learning in mixed groups as children from different primary backgrounds enter Year 7.

See Appendix 2 for examples of materials to support this event

- certificate of attendance
- passport
- vocabulary list
- flashcard games
- songs
- board game

- puppet workshop
- wordsearch
- dictionary quiz
- telling the story
- script of the interactive puppet show

---

6. Practical activities to support mixed-level classes in Key Stage 3

How do we take into account the fact that children are arriving in secondary school from a large number of different primary schools, with different levels of foreign-language acquisition? How can we manage transition in mixed-level groups and still ensure continuity and progression, while avoiding demotivation?

Dr Cynthia Martin (Martin 2000) listed the following solutions (NB we have added further details in italics):

- **Making a separate class for beginners**
  This may be achieved through block/mini-block timetabling, when pupils are mixed for all subjects but several classes come to the foreign language at the same time and are re-distributed according to their primary foreign language.

  For example, where Year 7s may be blocked in two halves on the timetable, in tutor groups, i.e. block A does MFL while block B does another subject. This enables the MFL department to remix the classes into sets, which can be organised according to the children's experience of the foreign language at primary school. By building on the children's prior language learning, teachers can provide continuity and progression.

- **Beginning a topic new for everyone**
  You could present a new topic during two of the three weekly lessons, e.g. 'Pocket money': How much? Who provides it? What is it spent on? In the third lesson, the support teacher could assist those new to the language, while pupils with prior knowledge of the language work through topic packs which revise and extend primary themes.

  Secondary teachers will need to think hard about re-planning and resourcing the Year 7 curriculum, to take into account the emerging primary languages scene. One idea is to produce new topic packs, perhaps using secondary MFL student teachers during their short (3–4 week) placement at the end of the year's PGCE course, when they have passed their practical teaching at the end of May. As a valuable further development or enrichment placement, these postgraduate students could put together extension or differentiation packs for secondary colleagues to use with pupils from primary who have language skills already. Such a task would also make a worthwhile project for a joint primary/secondary INSET, with primary teachers involved in seeing how their pupils would move on.

- **Actively targeting the newcomers without primary language experience during the first term (or year) of secondary school**
  - Deploying a learning support teacher who can speak the language during say, one of the three weekly lessons to provide catch-up work.
  - Another adult with language skills takes out beginners' group for one period a week.
  - Another adult with language skills takes out small group in class.

- Group teaching without support teachers.

  Pupils new to the foreign language will be unlikely to catch up on several years' of work in one term (although it may be several years, in most areas, before we are in this position), but should benefit from small group work with a teacher, with an improved pupil-teacher ratio allowing for rapid confidence-building and fast progress. The children will become familiar with language-learning strategies and activities, and should be able to acquire enough core knowledge of the topic areas previously covered in the primary school (such as greetings, personal information, numbers, etc) to participate enjoyably in whole-class lessons. This provides a means of differentiation, as meanwhile the rest of the class (with prior language knowledge) can progress through extension and enrichment activities on the same broad topic areas. If it is not possible to provide Foreign Language Assistants or additional teachers with foreign-language knowledge during timetabled sessions, a lunchtime 'catch-up' club could be a solution.

- Starter course including taped material to allow pupils to work on their own.

  Various CD-ROMs are available, based on the basics such as numbers, colours, who you are, etc. These include Pilote interactive, Petit pont *and the BBC websites* **www.bbc.co.uk/schools/primaryfrench** *and* **/primaryspanish**. *Pupils may need to be given access to tape recorders and computers.*

- Pairing pupils with a partner/partners for an initial period to work collaboratively.

  Using the 'buddy' system (see 'Some basic principles' below), pupils with previous knowledge of the foreign language can work alongside and support those without.

- **Coursebooks**
  - Changing to a new coursebook in secondary school.
  - Starting secondary coursebooks at a later unit.
  - Starting the coursebook at the beginning, but extending and recycling language.
  - Using the coursebook more selectively.

    Coursebooks can help in a variety of ways: changing to a new course can add interest by recycling the same content in new contexts. The books and their associated resources, such as videos and audio tapes, can be dipped into and used selectively for extension and enrichment.

- **Changing methods of assessment**
  For example:
  1 *Assess Year 7 Speaking by asking the children to pass a soft toy around a circle or group and say three sentences about themselves.*
  2 *Give Year 6 a Listening quiz designed to assess if they have reached Level 2.*

It is hoped that the *Key Stage 3 Strategy* will be revised to dovetail with the *Key Stage 2 Framework*, thus supporting continuity and progression of skills and learning acquired in the primary school, e.g. building on the children's understanding of grammatical terms. The Key Stage 2 Framework will have an impact on careful planning in Key Stage 3: secondary teachers will need to review their approach and content, and not merely repeat Key Stage 2 work and methodology. They should add breadth as they revisit language areas (see 'Some basic principles' below). They should choose fresh learning activities that are interesting and motivating, that build on pupils' prior learning in the same topic area and that extend across the four skills.

Continuity of experience can be developed through simple things like a familiar environment, familiar faces, similar games, songs, materials and resources; using the same classroom vocabulary or making a classroom display of work carried out in the primary school, to be

---

'The body'

- Key Stage 1: Finger rhymes (see Young Pathfinder 6: *Let's join in* (Martin and Cheater 1998) and ResourceFile 6: *Rhythm and rhyme* (Martin 2002))
- Key Stage 2: Sing 'Head, shoulders, knees and toes', play 'Beetle' (see Young Pathfinder 2: *Games and fun activities* (Martin 1995)) and progress to using the language in different contexts such as a game of 'Simon says', or primary topic areas to do with the body, such as health, where displays might be labelled in the foreign language
- Key Stage 3: There can be progression to discussing aches, pains and sporting injuries, and visiting the doctor or hospital

---

followed up in Year 7 (see discussion in Chapter 2: 'Familiarity of context', 'Continuity of simple language', etc and Appendix 2 for games ideas). For example:

At KS3 pupils need to progress to use all of the four skills. For example, personal details: children who have done little or no writing, but are familiar with text cards of key phrases about themselves, can be introduced to passages of text where children from the culture of the target language talk about themselves; they adapt these texts in order to write about themselves. Children used to arrive at Marple Hall School having had just one lesson of French per week at primary school in Year 6 and with some familiarity with text cards of key phrases of personal details, but having written a minimal amount (filling in one or two words on worksheets). They were able to progress, after only six weeks in Year 7, to word-processing a full A4 page about themselves for an open-evening display.

Increasingly, children will already have been using the four skills by the end of the primary phase and teachers will need to find new and stimulating contexts for recycling the language, such as using songs for sequencing and rewriting text creatively.

The following examples of practical activities can provide differentiation and develop continuity and progression, challenging the most able while providing the support that will allow pupils new to language learning to feel comfortable and willing to participate.

SOME BASIC PRINCIPLES

- Reinforce language which was introduced in the primary school, in a **new context** or activity in order to challenge the pupils to whom the language is familiar, while giving adequate support to new learners. This can be as simple as choosing an activity not used in the primary school (see 'Telephone directory' game below), or one more ambitious, e.g. to reinforce and broaden language associated with personal information: plan a 'TV programme' in which children interview famous personalities (working in groups or pairs and having first researched the answers, planned the questions and rehearsed the roles). New questions can be dealt with as they arise. The full 'programme' might become a magazine also containing songs and news, and could be performed at a school assembly or videoed for showing at an open evening.

- **Differentiate** by having a carousel lesson once a week: you could use this to focus on the beginners and give those with prior experience something different, e.g. a taped listening task – these are rare in primary, so would be something new for pupils even if they knew the content. You could, of course, also do this the other way round and give the beginners one set of tasks while you concentrate on those with languages experience. Many secondary courses come with such a wealth of material, including tapes, CDs and IT, that it should be possible to find alternative listening or pair-work tasks which could be drawn upon to extend some of the early chapters. Some courses for Year 7 now have differentiated coursebooks and with increasing demand more may become available. Foreign Language Assistants in secondary school could work either with the beginners or the experienced language learners.

- Introduce new language using **familiar techniques** and activities that are motivating but reassuring to Year 7 pupils. This assumes some liaison and joint planning between Key Stages, to acquire knowledge of the techniques already in use, as discussed in Chapters 1 and 2. Using favourite familiar techniques saves classroom time and these can be updated or adapted to the age group where necessary. A familiar technique might be the use of 'guessing': a teacher conceals or reveals only a small piece of an item for pupils to guess, e.g. a piece of realia or a number card, or a piece of text such as a sentence or question. At primary school, the children will be familiar with the use of flashcards and, in some cases, the interactive whiteboard; at secondary level the technique can be continued with the OHP or whiteboard, for example cutting up OHTs in an activity aimed at resequencing text. It is especially motivating when the child, pair or group who has guessed correctly is rewarded by taking the teacher's place and setting up the next piece of language to be guessed by the group.

- It is essential to know which pupils have some knowledge of the language: you can have quick access to a **record of prior language learning** by putting colour-coded dots in the register beside the names of these pupils. You could seat the class accordingly, giving each 'new' learner a more experienced neighbour, i.e. the 'buddy' system. Helping a partner with less language, or whose primary foreign language was different, gives a sense of responsibility to pupils with prior language learning and at the same time this provides them with valuable reinforcement in the language.

- Use the pupils with prior knowledge as '**language leaders**' – this makes them feel valued and, even if they are repeating things they have learned, at least their prior experience has been noticed, e.g.:
  - the confident pupil can partner the teacher to 'model' activities, i.e. the pupil acts as partner B while the teacher acts as partner A and they demonstrate role plays, games and activities together;
  - encourage pupils to take the role of the teacher, to volunteer for tasks such as calling the

numbers in Bingo, or to exemplify new language to the class;

- organise the class to work in **teams, groups or pairs** and encourage the 'leaders' to take the central role in group activities and role plays, e.g. as the scribe in an information-gathering exercise, or the interviewer in an imaginary TV studio. In this way, the classroom activities provide progression as well as differentiation – the core language is used by all; the 'language leaders' practise the new or extended language, as can other pupils once they feel confident to do so;

- provide progression as well as a sense of responsibility by allotting higher-level tasks to the 'language leaders', e.g. record new language and compile a class dictionary using ICT; be a 'language monitor' responsible for remembering specific items of classroom language for the class, such as how to ask for a pencil.

• When revisiting known language add something new in every lesson – a **'value-added' element**, to prevent demotivation ('We've done this already, miss!') while supporting 'new' learners, e.g.:

1 Names:
In KS2 children may learn '*Ich bin Heidi*', at KS3 they can broaden their knowledge and use '*Mein name ist Heidi*' – this will add a new structure for the pupil who has learnt the first phrase, while allowing 'new' learners to participate on equal terms.

2 Where I live:
Prior learning in KS2, '*J'habite à Portsmouth*'
New language in KS3, add a choice of dwellings:
Question: '*Tu habites dans un pub, un bungalow, un bateau, un wigwam, un appartement, une maison, ou une tente?*'
Answer: '*J'habite dans un pub!*'

• Use a **familiar context** in a challenging way, such as story-telling: continue work with a story in which they have taken part at KS2, using activities that extend their knowledge and develop their skills in a way that is suitable for KS3, e.g.

- provide pictures of the story mixed with other pictures for pupils to select from and sequence, then re-tell the story (this could be done in a group);

- re-tell sections with deliberate mistakes for the pupils to correct; re-write sections, with errors for them to correct;

- identify specific grammar elements: find adjectives, antonyms, cognates, false friends;

- put the key vocabulary into alphabetical order a) by first letter b) by first two letters;

- use a foreign-language dictionary to find meanings;

- use a foreign-language thesaurus to find alternative words;

- change the meaning of a section of the story by changing an adjective;

- provide an incomplete text of the story for pupils to replace missing words;

- pupils create a script for a small section of the story that you and the class have expanded; recycle the same structures and language into new plays;

- using a vocabulary list from the story, invent rhymes and raps and acrostics;

- brainstorm a list of characters, using these to create a story round the room;

- tell a story, while pupils take notes; they then produce a summary of it; they tell parts of the story relating to a chosen character; they then retell the story;

- pupils use random word cards to create a new story, intended to be narrated to children in KS2 (pupils must use each word).

- Provide activities in the four skills and list **items to focus** on, such as letters of the alphabet or numbers, e.g. higher maths: pupils have a list of numbers they must listen out for in some maths calculations, ticking off specific numbers each time they hear them (these can range from easy to more difficult numbers). At the end of the session, compare the numbers of times pupils think they have heard the numbers. A similar activity can be carried out with pupils listening out for specific letters of the alphabet during the spelling of addresses.
- Provide crib sheets of current vocabulary: ostensibly for new pupils this also provides good progression into **all four skills**, particularly reading and writing for everyone, especially the less able. They can be used as reference sheets in class and as the basis for homework, for activities such as quizzes and learning vocabulary.

 ## IDEAS FOR CLASSROOM ACTIVITIES

The activities listed below are particularly helpful for teachers faced with a mixed group in Year 7 as they do not depend on individual responses. All the activities are either **whole-class** or **team games** – in which all the class can be included and can **support one another**, or activities that can be carried out, for mutual support, in **pairs or groups** (e.g. two or more people working together, to prepare lists or to play a game of Bingo). They provide revision and recycling of known language for learners familiar with the language, while reinforcing it for new language learners. On the whole, the activities increase in difficulty, the last activities in each section requiring a higher level of language. To avoid over-competitiveness in team activities, keep the rewards simple, such as winning the right to the next turn. Wherever possible, encourage pupil volunteers to take over the teacher's role.

NUMBERS

- **Odds and evens**: The teacher calls numbers at random, girls jump up for even numbers, boys jump up for odd. All are able to join in quickly as they watch out for the reactions of their peers. Progress to the teacher holding up text cards of numbers without saying the numbers. Note: If you have a single-sex class, you could differentiate by birthday months.
- **Head numbers**:
  1 With their eyes closed everyone traces the shape of the numbers 0–9, moving their heads only.
  2 Then a volunteer calls out numbers in the foreign language, which everyone makes together, working with partners when it is necessary to produce two-digit numbers.
  3 Finally, in pairs, facing each other, one partner makes a number and the other partner tries to guess it.
- **Body numbers**: Each person finds a space to stand:
  1 A volunteer calls out numbers in the foreign language and pupils make the numbers using the whole of their bodies; they should hold the shape until another number is called.
  2 In pairs facing each other, one partner makes a number and the other partner tries to guess it.

3   In pairs: Partner A traces a number or letter on B's backs with a finger. If B guesses correctly he or she takes the next turn.

4   Join into groups of four – the pairs take it in turns to make two-digit numbers with their bodies, e.g. 51, 17 etc, for the other pair to guess.

•   **Show me**: Each pair or group of pupils has a set of small of digit cards, 0–9; the teacher calls a number, e.g. 14. First the pupils select and keep the number concealed, then on your signal all show you their number. This is good for informal assessment as you can see instantly any children showing an incorrect number, without their peers seeing too. Groups could compete to hold up two-digit numbers which must be presented to the class the correct way round, e.g. sixty-one = 61. You can progress to playing with individuals holding up correct two-digit numbers.

•   **Competition calculation**: Teams make up sums to ask each other – volunteers from each team answer for their team.

•   **Bingo**: Pupils can play in pairs (i.e. sharing a grid) and there are many variations on this game, e.g. using other items, such as letters of the alphabet. To play, the pupils need an empty grid of six squares. Give the class a set of numbers, e.g. even numbers to 30 and let them choose six to enter into their grid. Once the game begins you can ensure that no one is left behind, by displaying the numbers and asking volunteers to point to each number that you call, or by asking volunteers to write them up on the board – after a short pause to give everybody the time to try to identify it. You could progress to Maths or Prices Bingo, the teacher saying the calculations, the answers to which are numbers on the pupils' grids:

-   *Two-part bingo*: Part A (a disguised test) – the teacher calls out twelve numbers (or sums or verbs) and pupils try to list them correctly. Part B – having checked that all have the correct numbers, pupils use only numbers from this list to write in the Bingo grid, before playing the game;

-   *Tear-off bingo*: give each pupil a strip of A4 paper, which they must fold or concertina into eight sections. They write the selection of numbers in the eight squares. When numbers are called pupils can tear off or fold over only numbers showing on either end of the strip. Continue until a pupil shouts 'Bingo!' when his or her last number is called. If not torn into separate cards, pupils can exchange sheets and play again.

You can reuse the cards in an active game: pupils choose one card to hold; as the teacher calls our their number they stand, holding up their card; the last person left sitting wins. When everybody is standing, reverse the activity; a pupil can take over calling the numbers.

•   **Cheat!**: Play in pairs, using the separated 'cards' from the game above. Pupils keep their own pile of cards face down: Partner A takes a card from his or her pile and says a number, while keeping the card concealed; B must guess if this is true or false. The card is then revealed. If B guessed correctly, he or she keeps the card and takes the next turn. If incorrect, he or she returns the card and A has another turn. The player who gains all the cards is the winner. The cards can also be re-used to play Pelmanism.

•   **Telephone directory**: Each pupil, or pair, is given a number (these can range from two-digit numbers to full telephone numbers, as you feel is appropriate to the class) which they must keep secret. They jot down the initials of each member of the class with a space next to the initials for writing down the number. The teacher calls out the numbers one at a time. The pupil whose number is called replies '*Allô oui!*'. The teacher, or a volunteer, asks '*Qui est à l'appareil?*' The pupil answers with his or her name. The rest of the class write that number next to the pupil's name. Eventually the class has a complete 'directory' of everyone's number. This game may require much encouragement and repetition of the numbers, but is excellent for encouraging listening skills; to provide extra support the numbers could be held up each time by the teacher, after a pause to allow the children time to think for themselves.

- *Le grand jeu de nombres* (takes 10–15 minutes): Number each pupil round the class, then draw a quick numbered plan of the class. The teacher calls out a number, that pupil jumps up and calls another number, and so on. Pupils are out if they don't jump up at the correct moment when their number is called, or call out a number that is already 'out' of the game, or call back a person who has just called them. The teacher then crosses the numbers off the plan and the last one (or two) left in the game wins.

- **Higher maths**: Pupils have a list of numbers or letters they must listen out for in a Maths session of equations or other calculations. They tick them off their list every time they hear the numbers. At the end of the session compare the numbers of times pupils think they have heard the numbers.

PERSONAL INFORMATION AND ASKING QUESTIONS

- **What's my name?**: If you wish to use new names, and the class has not been provided with foreign-language names, write up a list of famous names related to the foreign language, e.g. Napoléon, etc. Partners secretly choose a name and write a name-tag which they then fix to their partner's back (either by folding over the paper and sticking it down the back of their jumper or by using double-sided tape). All pupils then circulate, asking yes/no questions to find out their 'name', e.g. '*Je m'appelle Joséphine?*'. When they have guessed the name on their back the teacher gives them another tag. The pupil who collects the most tags is the winner (the prize could be to choose a favourite game to finish the lesson).

- **Who are you?** (aimed primarily at new classes; potential for use of the 'third person'): Pupils write their full name on a slip of paper. Papers are collected and redistributed. Everyone circulates, asking a simple question to find the person whose name they hold. When they have found this partner they introduce them to the group, using either the third person or '*Voici ...*'. Extension: Ask the partner a few questions about him- or herself or his or her hobbies and mention these when presenting the pupil to the group.

- **The basket of names**: This works best in groups of about eight; a 'language leader' might be the 'teacher' in each group. The teacher gives his or her own name; the pupil on the left of the teacher points at the teacher saying, e.g. '*Voici Madame Brown*', then at him- or herself, giving his or her own name. Continue in this way, until the whole group has had a turn, giving the names of all the people sitting on their right before introducing themselves. After the whole group has had a go, start the process again. Extension: More complex structures such as the third person, e.g. '*Elle s'appelle Madame Brown*'.

- **Pop the question**: The class calls out questions in unison, for mutual support. Three volunteers stand at the back of the room while the class closes its eyes. Choose one of the volunteers to call a greeting or other item such as '*J'ai les yeux bleus*'. The whole class then calls out the question '*Qui est-ce?*'. The teacher tells the class the name of the pupil, e.g. '*C'est/Elle s'appelle Claire*', but this may be true or false, and the class must decide whether the teacher has told the truth: the class could chant '*vrai*' or '*faux*' in unison, with thumbs up or down, or choose a volunteer to answer. If the guess is successful, a pupil from the body of the class changes places with the volunteer whose name was guessed. This game can be used to practise other questions and phrases about themselves; it is an enjoyable and stress-free way of reinforcing the asking of questions.

- **That is the answer!**: This can be a team game for points. Write one word on the board; pupils ask you as many appropriate matching question(s) as possible, e.g.
  - Answer: '*Claire.*'
  - Questions: '*Qui est-ce?*'/'*Qui est derrière Simon?*', etc.
- **ID cards**: Working in pairs, pupils interview each other and fill in the answers on an ID card. The teacher may take some of the ID cards and read them out, omitting the names for the class to guess the identities. Some children can introduce their partner to the class using the information. Progression can be achieved here by the skilled language learners introducing their partners in the third person. Each pupil could draw a portrait on their card which could then be used for display.
- **Secret message**: The teacher writes a sentence or two to describe a spy in the class and shows the message to one pupil for a few seconds only. It then has to be passed secretly around the class, each pupil seeing it for a few seconds before writing it for his or her neighbour, while the lesson continues. Compare the end result with the original! Some of the class could read out their versions. It would be good if the spy turned out to be someone in the school or someone famous. This is a fun way of introducing written language.
- **This is me**: The following, progressively difficult, activities could be the culmination of work on personal details; they could be used for informal assessment. First ensure that the necessary language has been revised and, preferably, is displayed in support of the activities. As usual, pupils can carry out the activities in pairs:
  1 Each pupil, or pair, writes down on a slip of paper one sentence which will serve to identify them. These slips are folded and redistributed. Pupils move around (with partners), asking questions based on what is on their slip of paper in order to find the person described.
  2 Pupils draw a label about themselves, to stick on the front of their own jumper, then circulate and try to decipher each other's labels. They could use the first or second person, as appropriate to their level of knowledge.
  3 Progress to pupils secretly noting down three to five personal details, e.g. hobby likes/dislikes. Next, they try to find any partners with an identical list, using only the foreign language; they then keep circulating and try to become the largest group. You may like to discuss the outcome briefly with the class!
  4 Each pupil writes down five personal details, including a hobby, which would give a detective clues as to their identity, but leaving out their name. The slips of paper are mixed up and redistributed in pairs. Pupils try to identify who wrote the two lists they share. To see if they are correct they can then progress to interviewing anyone they think may correspond with the details on their paper.
- **Lie detector**: This activity can be based on a specific topic area, e.g. pets, or a wider theme such as personal details. A volunteer leaves the room and the class works together to decide on a set of questions to ask in the foreign language; the teacher or another volunteer writes

them on the board. The volunteer returns and answers all questions truthfully except one. The class must decide which answer is false.

- **That is the question!**: Pupils write down five questions they would like to be asked (these can be copied from questions previously written on the board). They then swap partners, exchange sheets and interview each other. Depending on their ability in writing, the answers could be noted down for later class discussion.

UNIVERSAL

- **Higher mime**: Introduce this by revising the basic 'Guess the mime' game (see Appendix 2) in which the class must guess a mime performed by a volunteer. Variations:

  1 *Collect a mime*: Groups watch other groups' mimes, writing them down (in the foreign language) until all are collected, e.g. food, pains, pets, or other theme chosen by the teacher.

  2 *Chain mime*: one pupil mimes an item of vocabulary, e.g. something to eat; others join in – when about ten have joined in, on a signal from the teacher they must call out what they are miming and the whole class can then join in the mime.

  3 *Working in groups*: Each group decides on something to eat or drink and works out a mime. The groups then dissolve and each person (or pair) finds someone from another group with whom to exchange mimes; they jot down the items when guessed. The mimes can be commented on or discussed critically at the end (first remind pupils of suitable language, e.g. *bien, excellent, pas bien*).

  4 *Work in groups of three*: Partner A chooses an item or phrase and whispers it to B, who mimes it to C, who tells A what he or she thinks it is. If C is successful, C chooses an item or phrase. This can be adapted to more players, e.g. D writes it for A. (If you wish the children to work in pairs you will need double the number of group members.)

- **Draw it**: Work in groups, each group having a scribe, with paper and pencil. The teacher whispers an item to one pupil from each group who then goes to a neighbouring group, which must guess the item as he or she draws it. As soon as they guess correctly, and one of the group has written it down, the artist goes back to the teacher for another item. The winning group is the first to guess five items. Variation: Number the pupils and have four new artists each time.

- **Secret signal** (*Chef d'orchestre*): A 'guesser' leaves the room while you choose the 'secret signaller'. The children chant a phrase from a short list of phrases on the board, e.g. dates, changing to the next phrase on the list as the secret signal is given. The guesser must guess the identity of the secret signaller by watching the class. This is a good activity for practising new or recycled text items – the children think they are shouting out phrases in a game, not just reading items aloud correctly several times over.

- **Correct me**: The class follows a text while the teacher, or a volunteer, reads it aloud – this could be a set of paragraphs about French children, a letter from a French pupil, or a story about a French child, for example. The teacher makes deliberate mistakes and pupils stop the teacher immediately as they notice them, e.g. '*Excusez-moi, Monsieur, c'est "onze" ans, ce n'est pas "dix" ans!*' The class could go on to repeat the activity in groups or pairs, one child taking the role of the teacher.

- **Nonsense!**: Work with a partner. Read a text and try to guess what the imaginary words mean, e.g. '*Je m'appelle Claire et j'ai dix … [imaginary word]*'. Have a class discussion at the end of the activity to allow all to complete the task if they have not done so, or use the activity as a competition and award points.
- **Group anagrams**: Work in groups. **Word** level: Each group chooses a scribe; on each table is a jumbled set of letter cards that make a word. The group unjumbles the words for the scribe to record; after two minutes, when the teacher gives the signal, they rejumble the words for the next group and then move on to another table. Progress to **sentence**, then **text** level.
- **Giant crossword**: Provide each group with a set of words, e.g. months of the year, on both horizontal and vertical cards. Pupils manipulate the words to create a crossword; they can use each word once only and tick off the words on an accompanying list, as they are used up. The resulting crossword may be copied on to squared paper and photocopied to provide crossword puzzles for homework. *Extension*: Make up clues for the crossword.
- **Split sentences**: Cut in half, sentences containing language known to the children. Give each pupil half a sentence and allow a minute or so for memorisation; they then circulate, saying them aloud, to find as many partners or combinations as possible, i.e. anyone whose half-sentence could fit before or after their own. Discuss possible combinations and eventually the correct solutions with the class – pupils must be able to justify combinations in order to claim them. After a few minutes, those with partners move to the side and those in the middle call out to the remaining group; two or three people may be found that fit. This works well with sentences from dialogues, e.g. '*Comment tu / t'appelles?*'. Groups can progress to reforming whole conversations on the board – anything that works gains a point.
- **Story**: Cut a short story into sentences. Each group is given a line or a dialogue to memorise and the strips are then collected. The class must now form into the correct sequence without writing. This could then be presented as a dialogue or play, adapted and added to, and eventually written out.
- **Lucky dip**: Teams brainstorm the vocabulary in a topic area. Now write each **word** on a slip and put it in an envelope, then exchange with another team. They then take turns to pick out a word and use it to make a correct **sentence** – pupils may help each other. The sentences are written up on the board or the OHP for the class to see and discuss. If all agree that the sentence is correct, the team keeps that slip. The team with the most slips wins.
- **Body words**: Work in groups of six to eight; each group has to find a word familiar to the class with the same number of letters as people in the group. Each person then forms one of the letters with his or her body and the group, as a whole, presents a visual interpretation of the entire word for the other groups to guess. Note: This is a lively activity and may require more space than the average classroom! The chosen 'words' could be prepared away from the classroom, perhaps as part of a homework. Variations:
  1 The class is divided into small groups (three or four); each group thinks of a word containing at least six letters and forms the first or last three letters of the word. The observers must try to guess the word.
  2 Working in groups of five or six proceed as in the original activity, but this time they jumble up the letters in their visual interpretation.
  3 Each group is given a slip of paper with a word which is difficult to spell or pronounce (as per **1**), some letters may be omitted.

REFLECTION

In this chapter we have provided a variety of suggestions for techniques and activities to help secondary teachers ensure a smooth transition in language learning for Year 7 pupils. By building on prior learning in a supportive and motivating way, teachers can provide continuity and linguistic progression for children who have already acquired language-learning skills in their primary schools, while including pupils with no previous knowledge of the foreign language.

Conclusion

In this book we have addressed the key issues surrounding transition from Key Stage 2 to Key Stage 3 in language learning. The current period of time, before entitlement in 2010, will perhaps prove the most difficult, as the *Key Stage 2 Framework for Languages* takes root in primary schools and secondary MFL departments are working out a way to cater for a wide diversity of prior knowledge and skills in Year 7. As the critical mass of pupils learning a language in Key Stage 2 increases, and eventually reaches 100%, the need for secondary teachers to have a clear knowledge of what level of achievement has been reached will be more acute. It will be necessary to differentiate their teaching, perhaps considering fast-track or early GCSEs.

We have suggested that the *European Language Portfolio* or similar record of achievement is used as a tool for transfer of information between the two phases. As the Languages Ladder becomes established as a way of measuring success in any language-learning situation, teachers will be more easily able to build on what has gone before.

The most important piece of advice we would like to share is: please, do mind the gap, but also build the bridges and ensure that you do not remain in isolation, whether in primary or secondary schools. Get together in clusters or local areas and share good practice; establish common schemes of work; join forces for activities and celebrations; get together and put faces to names. Above all, put the pupil at the centre and make sure that his or her passage in languages is a smooth one, so that he or she is motivated to continue to learn languages and so become a better citizen in the plurilingual, multicultural global village in which we live.

EPIGRAPH

A question that is often asked, about current initiatives in 'early starting' of foreign-language teaching, is: 'What are the lessons we should learn from the great national feasibility study of early starting, the Pilot Scheme ("French from Eight")?'

This brave, pioneering scheme was launched by Sir Edward Boyle, the insightful Conservative Minister of Education, in 1963, with enthusiastic backing from nearly 100 LEAs and massive funding from the Nuffield Foundation. It was controversially abandoned (after ten years of trial and four changes of government) in 1974.

*The Pilot Scheme came up against some difficulties that Sir Edward and his advisers could not have foreseen in 1962/63. Among problems that could have been foreseen, however, but were never solved and from which we might learn important lessons now, I would put very high on the list, after some involvement with the Pilot Scheme throughout, the **transition, of early starters, across the 11+ gap**.*

That is why I welcome and commend this important Young Pathfinder *publication.*

Eric Hawkins CBE, Professor Emeritus, York University

Appendix 1: Sources of further information and support

CILT, the National Centre for Languages
www.cilt.org.uk

For information on:
- regional and national support
- Comenius Network
- curricular models
- conferences
- courses
- trainers
- Resources Library
- publications, e.g. *Young Pathfinder, ResourceFiles, Early language learning DVD, European Language Portfolio*
- Information sheets

**The National Advisory Centre on Early Language
Learning (NACELL)**
www.nacell.org.uk

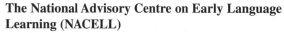

For information on:
- teaching foreign languages in primary schools
- continuing professional development, accredited courses and conferences
- *European Language Portfolio*
- Regional Support Groups
- *NACELL best practice guide*
- *Early language learning DVD: Making it happen, making it work and making it better*
- *Piece by piece: languages in primary schools*
- 'badged' resources
- e-mail discussion forums
- links to CILT, QCA and the DfES

Qualifications and Curriculum Authority (QCA)
www.qca.org.uk/ca/subjects/mfl/prim_schools.asp

For Guidelines and Schemes of Work:
- QCA Modern Foreign Languages non-statutory guidelines.
- *A scheme of work for Key Stage 2*
- Languages for young beginners: Reports and guides

Department for Education and Skills (DfES)

www.dfes.gov.uk

For National Strategy documents:
www.dfes.gov.uk/languages

- *Curriculum continuity: Effective transfer between primary and secondary schools*
- *Excellence and enjoyment: A strategy for primary schools*
- *Framework for teaching languages: Years 7, 8 and 9*
- *Languages for all: Languages for Life*
- *Key Stage 2 Framework for Languages*
- National Recognition Scheme: The Languages Ladder
- Schemes of work

BBC

www.bbc.co.uk

- Primary French and Spanish websites

Appendix 2: Resources

- Certificate of attendance
- Passport
- Vocabulary list
- List of flashcards
- Flashcard games
- Songs
- Board game
- Puppet workshop
- Wordsearch
- Dictionary quiz
- Telling the story
- Script of the interactive puppet show

SAMPLE CERTIFICATE OF ATTENDANCE

[logo ou drapeau]
Je constate que
[nom] ....
de ....
.... *[école]*
a assisté à une journeé
française, *[date]*
Signé ....
Le *[date]* ....

SAMPLE PASSPORT

Passeport pour

une journée française

A Ripon

mardi le 22 mai

10.00 à 15.00h

[Photo ou
dessin]

Nom . . . .

Age . . . .

Adresse

. . . .

. . . .

. . . .

Ecole . . . .

Anniversaire . . . .

Taille . . . .

Couleur de cheveux . . . .

Couleur des yeux. . . . .

Signé . . . .

VOCABULARY LIST

We chose the following examples because most of them are close to their English equivalents (cognates) and therefore easy to learn – and because we could find the soft toys to match! You can adapt the list to fit your own needs.

Le pique-nique
une limonade
un sandwich
un paquet de chips
une banane
une orange
du chocolat
une glace

Les animaux

un lion

une girafe

un éléphant

un kangourou

une araignée

un panda

un hippopotame

un toucan

un crocodile

un zèbre

un singe

un serpent

 ## FLASHCARD GAMES

You will need: Flashcards of zoo animals and picnic items (see lists above)

There are many games that are suitable for the introduction and learning of vocabulary. The following list can be added to with your preferred activities, or adapted to suit your own needs. Volunteers who guess items successfully can come to the front of the class to hold the flashcards.

- *Répétez et ajoutez* (Build-up): Introduce a few new items – repeat the first card, add one more, repeat the list from the beginning. Use voice modulation to vary this: whisper, shout, say it in a silly voice, mouth the items, rise to a crescendo, be happy, sad, angry, etc.
- *Indiquez* (Indicate): The teacher says an item – the children point to the appropriate card; progress to the teacher pointing to the card and the children saying the item.
- *Oui ou non?* (Yes or no?): Conceal an item behind your back, say what it is (or not) – the group must decide whether you are telling the truth. If they guess correctly, the class gains a point, e.g.

  Teacher (conceals an elephant): *C'est une girafe, oui ou non?*
  Group: *Oui!*
  Teacher: *Non, c'est un éléphant! Un point pour le professeur!*

- *La ola* (Mexican wave): Pupils stand up in turn and each call out an item in a short sequence (of three or four items), e.g. *un sandwich!/une limonade!/du chocolat!*
- *Flash!*: The group tries to guess the flashcard from seeing:
  – a quick flash;
  – a small corner;
  – a piece peeping through a keyhole cut in an envelope;
  – a card held upside down.

- *Devinez* (Guess it): The group tries to guess:
  - something held behind the teacher's back;
  - which card comes next on top of a pile.
- *Le jeu de Kim* (Kim's game): Volunteers act as card-holders at the front of the group. Ask the other children to shut their eyes while you turn one card away from them or let one volunteer stick a card up his or her jumper; the group then tries to identify the missing item. Let volunteers come to the front, shut their eyes and try to remember each item.
- *Lancez la gomme* (Throw the rubber): Spread out the cards on a table, a volunteer comes to the front and says the card he or she wants, then throws a rubber at that card. He or she can only obtain the card if the rubber lands on it.
- *Pouces* (Thumbs up): This game is calming. Four volunteers hold up flashcards in front of the group, the rest obey the instructions to shut their eyes and stick their thumbs in the air (*'Fermez les yeux ... pouces!'*). The volunteers quietly go and each touch **one** other child on the thumb, before returning to the front. The group are then instructed to open their eyes and the four children who have been touched must stand up (*Levez-vous les pouces!'*). The teacher asks each of the four standing which flashcard item has touched them (*'Quelle carte t'a touchée?'*) and they try to guess correctly. If successful, they change places with the volunteer who touched them and take their turn holding the card at the front, ready to play the game. Ask the remaining volunteers (who were successful in avoiding detection and therefore stayed at the front) who they touched (*'Qui as-tu touché?'*); if they are unfamiliar with the names of the other children they can point. The teacher may be able to use this opportunity to reinforce names (*'C'est Paul?'*). The children will soon become familiar with the language used in the game as the teacher can use gesture to illustrate meaning.
- *Mimez* (Guess the mime): Show a card or whisper something secretly to a volunteer, who mimes it for the group to guess – they can all say it or point to the correct item. Variation 1) half the group mimes an item for the other half to guess. 2) play in pairs: one chooses a card and mimes it using hands only; if the other partner guesses it correctly, he or she takes the next turn.
- *Battez le professeur* (Beat the teacher): This is also known as *Répétez si c'est vrai* (Repeat if it's true). The teacher names an item and shows a card; if the teacher has got it right the class must all repeat the item to win a point. If the teacher has got it wrong, the class must remain silent to win a point. The teacher wins the points when the class is outwitted.
- *Dans mon panier* (In my basket): To win a point, the children:
  - name one item in the bag or basket;
  - ask for a set of items in the same order that the teacher has named them;
  - replace items in the basket in the same order that the teacher has named them (see *'La chanson des listes'* overleaf).
- *Mémoire* (I went to market ...): Play this in the traditional way, with the first child naming an item, the second repeating the first item and adding one of his or her own choice and so on, up to a maximum of six or eight items, e.g. *'Dans mon panier j'ai ...'*.

SONGS

You will need:

- Flashcards of animals and picnic items, or props of the items (see lists above)
- OHTs of the songs
- overhead projector

1 (Tune: 'Here we go round the mulberry bush')

Voici un lion et un éléphant
Un éléphant, un éléphant
Voici un lion et un éléphant
Un éléphant

Voici un singe et un kangourou
un kangourou, un kangourou
Voici un singe et un kangourou
Un kangourou

Voici un zèbre et un hippopotame … *etc*

Voici un toucan et un crocodile … *etc*

Voici une araignée et un serpent … *etc*

2 *'La chanson des listes'* – repetition of vocabulary
This repetition song is based on a traditional Spanish children's song, *'Una sardina'*. The teacher chants or sings the first line, as in a military marching song, and encourages the children to repeat it.

Dans mon panier … *Dans mon panier*
J'ai un pique-nique … *J'ai un pique-nique*
J'ai une limonade … *J'ai une limonade*
et un sandwich … *et un sandwich*
J'ai un paquet de chips … *J'ai un paquet de chips*
J'ai une banane … *J'ai une banane*
J'ai une orange … *J'ai une orange*
et du chocolat! … *et du chocolat!*

3 (Tune: 'If you're happy and you know it')

Si tu aimes le soleil frappe tes mains
Si tu aimes le soleil frappe tes mains
Si tu aimes le soleil, le printemps qui se réveille
Si tu aimes le soleil, frappe tes mains
Si tu aimes le soleil … tape tes pieds
                    claque tes doigts
                    dis 'Bonjour'
                    lève-toi
                    répète tout!

BOARD GAME

You will need:

- copies of the board
- game tick sheet
- pencil for each child
- dice
- counters for each small group (two to four children)

Le serpent: This is a version of 'Snakes and ladders', in which the players throw dice to travel around the outside of the board, visiting the zoo and collecting a picnic on the way. They follow the numbering on the spaces, but encounter obstacles on their way: these are indicated by arrows and numbers showing the direction to follow, generally back the way they have come, and how many steps to take, e.g. *3 pas* >>. If the players are unlucky and land on a snake's head they must follow the snake down its length to the tail, although they may be able to escape back on to the route halfway down (see board page 61).

Each time players land on a picnic item they 'collect' it, by ticking the item on a separate sheet. When they have ticked off the six items they can go straight to the square depicting the completed tick sheet and so to the picnic in the centre of the board.

The winner is the first to reach the picnic: players can draw in the basket on their sheet to show they have finished and could have a sticker placed on the basket at the bottom of the column. The sheet provides columns for three games. There is a further activity linking the words to the items. Pupils can keep their sheets at the end of the session.

The children should be encouraged to use French for playing the game, e.g. saying the number on the dice and counting with their counter; saying the animals and picnic items they land on. If appropriate, they could also be taught to say, *'C'est à toi/moi'*.

PUPPET WORKSHOP

You will need, for each puppet:

- photocopies of the snake head
- one clean sock per pupil
- double-sided tape
- scissors
- colouring pens or pencils

INSTRUCTIONS

- *Colorie le serpent ... colorie la tête, les yeux, la langue:* colour in the snake ... the head, the eyes, the tongue

- *Découpe-le*: cut it out (to avoid the use of scissors and the collection of litter, you may wish to prepare this activity in advance, providing each child with a pre-cut snake head)
- *Prends une chaussette, attache le serpent:* take a sock, stick the snake onto it (with double-sided tape)
- *Dialogue avec un partenaire:* have conversations with a partner

WORDSEARCH

WORDSEARCH: ANIMALS AND PICNICS!

Name ……………………………………………..

School ……………………………………….

S	A	B	W	K	A	N	G	O	U	R	O	U	E	R
F	I	C	R	O	C	O	D	I	L	E	E	Y	T	H
G	S	N	D	F	G	H	J	K	L	L	K	Z	X	I
T	L	M	G	M	E	G	N	I	S	N	B	V	C	P
E	W	A	T	E	L	E	P	H	A	N	T	M	B	P
B	G	F	C	P	I	Q	U	E	N	I	Q	U	E	O
U	H	H	J	E	D	F	G	H	D	Y	V	V	C	P
J	I	Y	T	H	R	E	G	D	W	C	V	N	B	O
X	P	Z	E	D	A	N	O	M	I	L	G	Z	X	T
Z	P	A	Q	U	E	T	D	E	C	H	I	P	S	A
E	O	E	R	R	T	Y	U	H	H	Y	R	A	M	M
B	P	Y	O	I	O	U	O	H	G	I	A	N	T	E
R	O	P	T	O	U	C	A	N	U	M	F	D	O	L
E	T	A	S	D	O	F	O	O	Z	J	E	A	U	M
R	A	Q	W	L	E	G	G	L	A	C	E	Y	K	M
S	M	D	A	F	O	R	A	N	G	E	I	O	A	E
C	E	T	R	L	T	Y	T	S	E	R	P	E	N	T
B	N	M	A	R	A	I	G	N	E	E	M	K	I	T

Trouvez ces mots:

ARAIGNEE
CHOCOLAT
CROCODILE
ELEPHANT
GIRAFE
GLACE
HIPPOPOTAME
KANGOUROU
LIMONADE
ORANGE
PANDA
PAQUET DE CHIPS
PIQUENIQUE
SANDWICH
SERPENT
SINGE
TOUCAN
ZEBRE
ZOO

Score:

© Ann Gregory

Solution

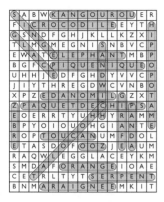

 DICTIONARY QUIZ

NB It is important that every child has the same edition and same dictionary for this quiz to work. Teachers will need to adapt the questions to fit the dictionary available.

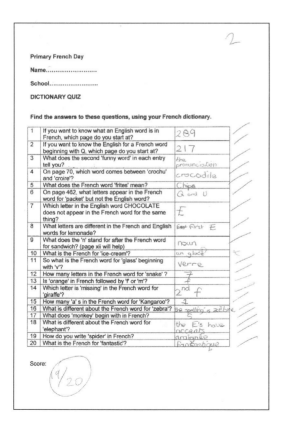

TELLING THE STORY

- You will need:
  - overhead projector
  - large screen
  - OHTs of zoo animals in the story (it is helpful to have an assistant to show these)
  - flashcards: animals, picnic items
  - text card signs: *zoo*; *glaces* (with illustrated price list, if possible)
  - soft toys of each zoo animal (see 'Vocabulary list' above)
  - picnic basket
  - 'zoo': box or crate to hold zoo animals
  - real or simulated picnic items: sandwich, orange, French crisps, French chocolate, lemonade
  - ice cream(s): tissue paper in a real cornet
  - lead or 'star' puppet(s), i.e. Bernard
  - cassette player
  - cassette of animal noises/sound effects (or have the children make the sounds)

- **The participants will need**: one snake sock puppet per child

- **Summary**: Today is Bernard's birthday outing to the zoo, but unfortunately he is frightened of snakes and at first he thinks that every animal is a snake. After 'visiting' each animal he wants his picnic, but first he has to finish walking round the zoo. The last animals he visits are the snakes and Bernard is so frightened he runs away, upsetting the picnic basket (behind the zoo box); when he comes back the basket is empty – the monkeys have eaten the picnic! But all ends well as he has an ice cream instead. (See script on page 89.)

  Note: Apart from the beginning and the ending of the story, the same scene is repeated each time as you introduce new animals, using the same language.

- **Action!**: Prepare the audience participation – begin with the 'French wave', i.e. when silence is signalled by putting your hand in the air, all must put their hands up and be quiet too – in this way silence will fall around the room, without having to raise your voice. Choose a few phrases that you will repeat often in the story and practise these with their accompanying actions, e.g.

  Oh regardez! . . . . shield eyes
  Ecoutez! . . . . cup ears
  Non! . . . . shake heads and point a finger
  Oui! . . . . nod and smile
  Qu'est-ce que c'est? . . . . raise hands in mock alarm and say '*oh-oh!*' or '*oh là là!*'
  le zoo . . . . walk fingers
  le pique-nique . . . . say '*miam miam*', rub tummy and mime drinking
  les serpents! . . . . hiss and wave puppets menacingly

- **Practise the song** (marching-type repetition chant or made-up song):

  Dans mon panier … *Dans mon panier*
  J'ai un pique-nique … *J'ai un pique-nique*

J'ai une limonade … *J'ai une limonade*
et un sandwich … *et un sandwich*
J'ai un paquet de chips … *J'ai un paquet de chips*
J'ai une banane … *J'ai une banane*
J'ai une orange … *J'ai une orange*
et du chocolat! … *et du chocolat!*

… *Alors, regardez* (shield eyes) … (replace items in the basket as you say them) … *dans mon panier j'ai une limonade, un sandwich, un paquet de chips, une banane, une orange et du chocolat.*

(If you have time, play games from the list above, e.g. let volunteers come to the front and name the items as they take them out of the basket, or replace items in the same order as you say them, see 'Flashcard games' above.)

Script of the interactive puppet show

Le pique-nique au zoo

• **Introduction**

Bernard greets the audience and then individuals around the room, '*Salut! Bonjour! Je m'appelle Bernard. Comment tu t'appelles? Ça va?*', etc.

Children could be encouraged to answer their own or their snake's name, e.g. '*Je m'appelle Sensass le Superserpent!*'

Tell the story with maximum audience participation (refer to the highlighted words and matching list of actions above), adapting the script to your own needs.

• **The story**

(Sound effect – music)

Scene 1

Narrator: Aujourd'hui c'est ton anniversaire, Bernard. *(If you wish, sing* 'Joyeux anniversaire', *ask the puppet his age, etc.)* Bernard, tu veux faire de la géographie/des mathémathiques?

Bernard: **Non!**

Narrator: Tu veux visiter **le zoo**? *(Point to zoo sign.)* **Oui** ou **non**?

Bernard: **Oh oui**, mais … il y a des **serpents**? Je n'aime pas les **serpents**!

Narrator: Oh **non** *(hide Bernard's eyes to shield him from the audience of hissing snakes)* au **zoo** ils sont sympa, les **serpents**!

Bernard: Ça va, alors! *(to audience)* On va au **zoo**? **Oui**?
            (Narrator encourages audience to agree.)

Narrator: *(Show picnic basket.)* **Qu'est-ce que c'est**?

Bernard: C'est un **pique-nique**?

Narrator: Oui. C'est un **pique-nique**!

Bernard:	Oh super! Moi, j'aime les **pique-niques**!
Narrator:	Bien, chantez avec moi …

Dans mon panier … *Dans mon panier*
J'ai un pique-nique … *J'ai un pique-nique*
J'ai une limonade … *J'ai une limonade*
et un sandwich … *et un sandwich*
J'ai un paquet de chips … *J'ai un paquet de chips*
J'ai une banane … *J'ai une banane*
J'ai une orange … *J'ai une orange*
et du chocolat! … *et du chocolat!*

… Alors, **regardez**, dans mon panier j'ai … *(hold up)* une limonade, un sandwich, un paquet de chips, une banane, une orange et du chocolat *(replace in basket)*.
… Oh **regardez**! *(Point to zoo sign.)* Voilà le **zoo**! Allons-y!

Scene 2 (to be repeated for each animal)

Narrator:	**Regardez**! *(Look around as a small piece of animal is revealed on OHP.)* **Qu'est-ce que c'est**? … **Ecoutez** … *(sound effect of a lion)* … C'est un hamster?
Bernard:	Ooh! … **Non**! C'est un **serpent**? Je n'aime pas les **serpents**! … *(Bernard hides his head from the audience of hissing snakes.)*
Narrator:	**Non**, ce n'est pas un **serpent**. *(Bernard recovers.)* C'est une girafe ou c'est un lion? *(Encourage the audience to answer.)* … Un lion! *(OHT – reveal lion.)* … **Oui**, c'est un lion!

(If you wish, question the audience further, with gestures to illustrate the language, before pulling the soft toy or flashcard from the zoo box, e.g.

… C'est un grand lion ou c'est un petit lion? C'est un lion jaune ou bleu?
… **Oui**, c'est un petit lion! C'est un petit lion jaune!)

(Reveal the animal, hand it to a volunteer who attempts to say it, and then bring him or her to stand at the front, to be joined by other animals later.)

… Viens ici! Voilà un petit lion jaune. Très bien! … Ça va Bernard?

Bernard:	Ça va très bien merci. J'aime les lions. Maintenant c'est le **pique-nique**?
Narrator:	**Non, non, non**! D'abord on visite le **zoo**, après c'est le **pique-nique**.
Bernard:	*(Gets more and more frustrated as the story progresses.)* **Ohhh**!

(Repeat this scene for each of your animals, varying it as you wish. As you give out each animal to volunteers, they gradually form a line at the front. You could sometimes go back down the line naming the animals and count up the animals at the end.)

Final scene

Narrator:	**Regardez**! *(Look around as a small piece of animal is revealed on the OHP.)* **Qu'est-ce que c'est? Ecoutez** …

... C'est un éléphant?

Bernard: Ooh! ... **Non**! C'est un **serpent**! **C'est un très, très grand SERPENT**! Je n'aime pas les **serpents**! *(Bernard runs away. Narrator then hands a snake to a volunteer as usual.)*

Narrator: *(Bringing Bernard back)* Alors. Ça va Bernard?

Bernard: **NON**! Je n'aime pas les **serpents**! Je n'aime pas le **zoo**!

Narrator: Mais maintenant c'est le **pique-nique**!

Bernard: Ça va alors! Super!

Narrator: *(Holds up empty basket.)* Oh **non**! Oh là là! *(sound effect of monkeys)* ... **Regardez**! Les singes ont mangé tout le **pique-nique**! ...

('Monkeys' could run across the front, each holding a picnic item and making monkey noises.)

Bernard: Bouhou! *(Encourage audience to cry, too.)*

Narrator: Oh **regardez**! Voilà des glaces *(pointing to GLACES sign)*. Tu aimes les glaces, Bernard?

Bernard: **OUI**!

Narrator: Très bien! Tu veux une glace?

Bernard: **OUI**!

Narrator: Quel parfum? Banane, fraise, vanille, chocolat?

Bernard: **Une grande glace au chocolat, s'il te plaît**.

Narrator: Voilà! *(Bernard eats the ice cream enthusiastically.)* ... Ça va Bernard?

Bernard: Oh **OUI**! Ça va très, très bien, merci! C'est extra!

Narrator: Alors, chantez avec moi *(repeat the song if wished, putting items back into the basket)*.

... Au revoir les **serpents**!

... Au revoir le **zoo**!

(Bernard bows out, encourage the volunteers holding the animals to do the same.)

(Sound effect – music)

References

Buckby, M. (1981) *Graded Objectives and tests for Modern Languages – an evaluation.* Schools Council.

Cheater, C. and Farren, A. (2001) Young Pathfinder 9: *The literacy link.* CILT.

CILT (2001, 2005) *European Language Portfolio.* CILT.

CILT (2003) *NACELL best practice guide.* CILT. (**www.nacell.or.guk/bestpractice**)

CILT, the National Centre for Languages (2005) *Early language learning DVD: Making it happen, making it work and making it better.* CILT, the National Centre for Languages.

Datta, M. and Pomphrey, C. (2004) Young Pathfinder 10: *A world of languages!: Developing children's love of languages.* CILT, the National Centre for Languages.

DfES (1998) *National Literacy Strategy.* DfES.

DfES (2002) *National Languages Strategy: Languages for all: Languages for life.* DfES.

DfES (2003a) *Excellence and enjoyment – A strategy for primary schools.* DfES.

DfES (2003b) *Framework for teaching modern foreign languages: Years 7, 8 and 9.* DfES.

DfES (2004) *Curriculum continuity: Effective transfer between primary and secondary schools.* DfES.

DfES (2005) *Key Stage 2 Framework for Languages.* DfES.

DfES/CILT (2004) *Piece by piece: Languages in primary schools.* CILT.

Driscoll, P. and Frost, D. (1999) *The teaching of modern foreign languages in the primary school.* Routledge.

Driscoll P., Jones, J. and Macrory, G. (2004) *The provision of foreign language learning for pupils at Key Stage 2. Research report.* DfES.

Farren, A. and Smith, R. (2003) *Bringing it home: How parents can support children's language learning.* CILT.

Gardner, R. C. and Lambert, W. E. (1985) *Social psychology and second language learning: The roles of attitudes and motivation.* Rowley Mass.: Newbury House.

Gregory, A. (1996) *Primary foreign language teaching: Influences, attitudes and effects.* University of Leeds (unpublished MEd thesis, available on loan from University of Leeds and York St John libraries).

Gregory, A. (2001) 'Primary foreign languages – the Key Stage 2–3 transfer point'. In: Chambers, G. (ed) Reflections on Practice 6: *Reflections on motivation.* CILT.

Hammerley, H. (1989) *French immersion: Myths and reality*. Calgary: Detselig Enterprises.

Harris, J. and Conway, M. (2002) *Modern languages in Irish primary schools: An evaluation of the national pilot project*. Dublin: Institiuid Teageolaiochta Eireann.

Johnstone, R. (1994) *Teaching modern languages in the primary schools: Approaches and implications*. Scottish Council for Research in Education.

Johnstone, R. (2003) 'Evidence-based policy: Early language learning at primary'. *Language Learning Journal* Winter 2003 28: 14–21.

Krashen, S. (1981) *Second language acquisition and second language learning*. Pergamon Institute of English.

Low, L., Brown. S., Johnstone, R. and Pirrie, A. (1995) *Foreign languages in primary schools: Evaluation of the Scottish pilot projects 1993–1995*. Final report. Scottish CILT.

Martin, C. (1995) Young Pathfinder 2: *Games and fun activities*. CILT.

Martin, C. (2000) *An analysis of national and international research on the provision of modern foreign languages in the primary school*. QCA.

Martin, C. (2002) ResourceFile 6: *Rhythm and rhyme: Developing language in French and German*. CILT.

Martin, C. and Cheater, C. (1998) Young Pathfinder 6: *Let's join in!: Rhymes, poems and songs*. CILT.

QCA (2000a) *Modern Foreign Languages: A scheme of work for Key Stage 2*. QCA.

QCA (2000b) *Modern Foreign Languages: A scheme of work for Key Stage 2 – Teacher's guide*. QCA.

QCA (2000c) *National Curriculum handbook for primary teachers in England: Key Stages 1 and 2*. QCA.

Rowe, I. and Kilberry, I. (2002) *Early Start Spanish: Mi ciudad y mi colegio*. Early Start Languages.

Satchwell, P. (1997) Young Pathfinder 4: *Keep talking*. CILT.

Satchwell, P. and de Silva, J. (2004) Young Pathfinder 11: *A flying start: Introducing early language learning*. CILT, the National Centre for Languages.

Singleton, D. (1989) *Language acquisition: The age factor*. Multilingual Matters.

Tierney, D. and De Cecco, J. (1999) *Modern languages in the primary school research: Final report*. University of Strathclyde.

Tierney, D. and Hope, M. (1998) Young Pathfinder 7: *Making the link*. CILT.

WEBSITES MENTIONED IN THE BOOK

CILT, the National Centre for Languages: www.cilt.org.uk

Common European Framework: www.culture2.coe.int/portfolio/documents_intro/common_framework.html

Content and Language Integration Project: www.cilt.org.uk/clip/index.htm

Development of Early Language Learning (DELL) projects: www.nacell.org.uk/happening/schools/dell.htm

Early Language Learning Regional Support Groups: www.nacell.org.uk/regional

European Language Portfolio – Junior version: www.nacell.org.uk/elp.htm

Key Stage 3 National Strategy: www.standards.dfes.gov.uk/keystage3

Languages Ladder: www.dfes.gov.uk/languages/DSP_languagesladder.cfm

MFL KS2 schemes of work: www.standards.dfes.gov.uk/schemes/primary_mfl/?view=get

MFL Programme of study: Key Stages 3 and 4: www.nc.uk.net

NACELL best practice guide: www.nacell.org.uk/bestpractice

NACELL resources: www.nacell.org.uk/resources/resources.htm

National Curriculum: www.nc.uk.net

Piece by piece: Languages in primary schools – 'Twelve questions you may want to ask': www.nacell.org.uk/cdrom/questions.htm

QCA – About Modern foreign languages: www.qca.org.uk/ca/subjects/mfl/prim_schools.asp

TRAFIC project: www.trafic.eu.com